TURN THE PAGE

HOW TO READ LIKE A TOP LEADER

READ RIGHT TO LEAD RIGHT

OBSTACLÉS
PRESS

First Edition, December 2013

10 9 8 7 6 5 4 3 2 1

Published by:
Obstaclés Press
4072 Market Place Dr.
Flint, MI 48507

www.life-leadership-home.com

ISBN 978-0-9895763-9-0

Cover design and layout by Norm Williams, nwa-inc.com

Printed in the United States of America

Today a reader, tomorrow a leader.
—Margaret Fuller

CONTENTS

INTRODUCTION

Reading is a voyage of discovery. In each book, paragraph, or even sentence, an unforeseen treasure may lie hidden. Sometimes these surprises make us laugh, and sometimes they make us cry; mostly, they make us think. The thrill of it all is in not knowing what to expect. Without warning, something great can pop off the page and lodge itself permanently in our memory, where it takes root and grows into an integral part of who we are.

I recently came across just such a treasure. I was browsing through an obscure novel I had purchased years before in a secondhand bookstore. Its historical setting and swashbuckling plot had caught my attention, and in a moment of relaxation, I snuck out by the lake and began reading merely for pleasure. I didn't expect anything great to come from such a fameless and unknown publication. In fact, I didn't expect anything at all. But then, within a few pages, I came across an extended quote from another book, written more than a century previously, by former slave Frederick Douglass:

> The more I read, the more I was led to abhor and detest my enslavers. I could regard them in no other light than a band of successful robbers, who left their homes, and gone to Africa, had stolen us from our homes, and in a strange land reduced us to slavery. I loathed them as being the meanest as well as the most wicked of men. As I read and contemplated the subject, behold! that very discontentment which Master Hugh had predicted would follow my learning to read had already come, to torment and sting my soul to unutterable anguish. As I writhed under it, I would at times feel that

learning to read had been a curse rather than a blessing. It had given me a view of my wretched condition, without the remedy. It opened my eyes to the horrible pit, but to no ladder upon which to get out. In moments of agony, I envied my fellow slaves for their stupidity. I have often wished myself a beast. I preferred the condition of the meanest reptile to my own. Any thing, no matter what, to get rid of thinking! It was this everlasting thinking of my condition that tormented me. There was no getting rid of it. It was pressed upon me by every object within sight or hearing, animate or inanimate. The silver trump of freedom had roused my soul to eternal wakefulness.

—*Narrative of the Life of Frederick Douglass, An American Slave* (1845), from *Classic Slave Narratives*, edited by Henry Louis Gates Jr.

Douglass's words cut me to the quick. More than 165 years later, I sat by the lakeshore full of remorse for Douglass and those like him who had endured such injustice.

I also marveled at the power of mere symbols on a page to convey such deep sentiment and emotion across the separation of time and place. The power of reading had been brought home to me through the eloquent words of Frederick Douglass. Interestingly, Douglass himself was marveling at this very same power. It was reading that had brought him to his painful self-awareness.

When you hear about reading, many different connotations may come to mind. Perhaps you think of entertainment, relaxation, passing the time, or even wasting time. Perhaps you think of reading as boring, or something you had to do in school and happily have to do no more.

If your thoughts about reading tend toward these neutral or even negative associations, you are not alone. According to statisticbrain.com, fully 50 percent of US adults are unable to read an eighth-grade-level book, while 33 percent of US high school graduates will never read a book again after high school. It is even worse with college students, where a full 42 percent will never read a book after college. Shockingly, 80 percent of US families did not buy a book this year, while 70 percent of adults have not been in a bookstore in the past five years! Finally, 57 percent of books are never read to completion.

Not only is this a chilling assessment of where our culture is these days, but it also may be a scary predictor of where it's heading. This is because most (if not all) of the greatest contributors to society and its progress have been voracious readers, with many of them citing specific books that changed their lives.

The founders of the United States were all, without exception, avid and habitual readers. Thomas Jefferson was such an avid reader that he was told by friends that he would ruin his eyesight if he continued reading so ferociously. He paid them no heed and uttered the famous line, "When I have money, I buy books, and if I have anything left over, I buy food."

Henry Knox was a bookstore proprietor before the American Revolution began. But he quickly rose to be one of George Washington's most trusted generals and learned all he knew about artillery through the frenzied reading of books on the subject.

Napoleon Bonaparte famously read all he could get his hands on as a youth and adolescent. Abraham Lincoln transformed himself from his humble beginnings into a pivotal American statesman largely through the power of reading.

Teddy Roosevelt, the youngest man ever to become a US president, was famous for reading in all situations and conditions. Once, out on his western ranch, a couple of rustlers stole his boat. In a sleeting winter storm, Roosevelt tracked the men upriver and finally apprehended them at gunpoint, forcing them to row his boat back to his ranch. Incredibly, he sat reading in the back of the boat during the trip, keeping a gun pointed at the outlaws the whole time!

Harry Truman, thirty-third president of the United States, never attended college. But he read so much he was equally as educated as the most highly lauded graduates of any school. It was Truman who said, "Not every reader is a leader, but every leader must be a reader."

Oprah Winfrey—actress, businesswoman, and advice-giver extraordinaire—was only allowed to watch one hour of television per day by her grandmother who raised her. To fill in the rest of the time, little Oprah engrossed herself in books. She is said to have had a novel and a self-help book going at all times right into adulthood.

Actor Matthew McConaughey attributes his entire career to the reading of a book. "I was enrolled at the University of Texas with the idea of studying law," he said. "But I wasn't sleeping well with that idea. I read the first two chapters of *The Greatest Salesman in the World*, and I knew right then that I wanted to go to film school. I changed my major the next day."

Singer, songwriter, and business mogul Jimmy Buffett once said that the greatest gift his mother gave him was a love for reading. Lou Holtz, one of college football's all-time winningest coaches, said the book *The Magic of Thinking Big* was a major turning point in his professional life.

Academy Award winner Donna Reed was an insecure high school freshman when she read the book *How to Win Friends and Influence People*, which she credited with inspiring her to continue learning to work with people so she could pursue her dream of acting.

This list could go on indefinitely because it has always been true that reading is one of the foundational cornerstones to living a successful life. Throughout history, seemingly everyone who accomplished anything knew this intrinsically. But somehow, today, we've drifted away from this truth.

This is strange when we consider that we now live in the "Information Age," in what some have dubbed the "Knowledge Economy." But yet, at the same time, the art of reading—and reading well—seems to be slipping from our culture.

Reading is the shortcut to knowledge and wisdom, a path to excellence, an exciting journey of learning, and it provides access to the greatest minds of human existence. In the words of one leader, reading is "having conversations with dead guys." Or as Isaac Newton said in a backhanded compliment to his rival Robert Hooke (who was extremely short), "If I have seen further, it is by standing on the shoulders of giants."

Reading provides all these advantages and more. It brings self-awareness, other awareness, a broader view and increased tolerance, a better attitude and deeper gratitude, understanding, and sharpness, and it can keep a reader both current with the times and up on the times that have passed.

Reading can keep us grounded and raise our dreams to the heavens at the same time. It can teach success as well as lead to significance. It provides and inspires thinking but also spurs one to action. And so much more!

When considering our lives and how to live them well, we can do little to provide more in terms of absolute growth and advancement than to develop an ongoing, productive, and lifelong habit of *leadership reading*.

Leadership reading is reading with a bent toward making the page impact our lives. It is more than just pleasure, although it can be immensely enjoyable. It is more than reading a lot of books, although it will certainly take us through many volumes.

Leadership reading is the active, intentional devouring of the greatest writings applied with earnestness toward the highest aspirations. It is a lifestyle habit that is open to everyone but taken advantage of by only a select few.

This book was written to help you become one of those few. May it inspire you to seek the best, apply it deeply, and live it widely.

Turn the page!

Chris Brady
New York Times Bestselling Author

> *The average salesman does not read a book a year;*
> *that is why he is the average salesman!*
> —Anonymous

PROLOGUE

Isn't it odd how much fatter a book gets when
you've read it several times? . . . As if something were
left between the pages every time you read it.
Feelings, thoughts, sounds, smells . . . and then when you
look at the book again many years later, you find yourself
there, too, a slightly younger self, slightly different,
as if the book had preserved you like a pressed
flower . . . both strange and familiar.
—Cornelia Funke

Leaders are readers, and great leaders are nearly always great readers. Atwood H. Townsend said, "No matter how busy you may think you are, you must find time for reading, or surrender yourself to self-chosen ignorance." Ignorance is not a position of strength, and it's a terrible foundation from which to launch a leadership revolution. Indeed, Mark Twain said, "A person who won't read has no advantage over one who can't read."

> Ignorance is not a position of strength, and it's a terrible foundation from which to launch a leadership revolution.

There is a connection between reading and leadership throughout history. Many of the biggest names in leadership are simultaneously big names in reading, and very often, men or women who achieve extraordinary leadership results stress the importance of reading and great books.

Thomas Jefferson is famous for his exclamation, "I cannot live without books!"

Frederick Douglass is known for such sayings as "Knowledge makes a man unfit to be a slave" and "Once you learn to read, you will be free forever." Napoleon Bonaparte said, "Show me a family of readers, and I will show you the people who move the world."

The list goes on. However, while it is true that real, effective leadership requires a level of intense readership, reading itself is not enough to transform the ordinary person into a powerful and impactful leader. In fact, there are many people who read for hours every day and never achieve real leadership results, even if they have leadership-oriented goals.

Leaders Read Differently

One of the main reasons for this is that top leaders read differently than most people. If more of us knew how to read the way leaders do, we'd be much more able to emulate their success.

What many people don't understand is that there are many *ways* to read. For example, students read to find out what a book says. They want to pass tests and get good grades on reports, essays, and presentations. Sometimes a book will pique a student's interest, and he or she will study with increased depth and passion. But the focus is usually still on what the book actually says. In contrast, scholars read seeking to find out either what the book could say or what it means. They get into the examination of word choice and consider multiple possible meanings. They research the author's history and background to determine the most likely meanings and intentions of his works, and they dig deeply into textual analysis.

While both of these reading styles have merit and may even accomplish

> If more of us knew how to read the way leaders do, we'd be much more able to emulate their success.

the goals of the reader, neither describes the way most top leaders read a book. As Gustave Flaubert said, "Do not read, as children do, to amuse yourself, or like the ambitious, for the purpose of instruction. No, read in order to live." Leaders are less concerned with the mere knowledge of a million facts than they are with the internalization and application of real principles and solutions. Leaders read to learn what they need to know, do, or feel, regardless of the author's intent or words. As they read, they search for answers to questions, great examples of leadership, and whatever else they may need in their leadership journey and mentorial relationships.

Get the Book through You

Ursula K. Le Guin expressed this point well when she said, "We read books to find out who we are. What other people, real or imaginary, do and think and feel . . . is an essential guide to our understanding of what we ourselves are and may become."

Mortimer J. Adler added to the conversation when he suggested, "In the case of good books, the point is not to see how many of them you can get through, but rather how many can get through to you."

> Leaders see past the words and read with the specific intent of finding truth and *applying* it directly in their own lives.

When asked what you are reading, if you can do nothing but reply with Hamlet, "Words, words,"[1] you are probably missing an important step in the way you approach books. To read for leadership, you have to learn to think like a leader. Leaders see past the words and read with the specific intent of finding truth and *applying* it directly in their own lives.

Learn to Read Like a Top Leader

The techniques and hands-on examples in this book on how to read like a leader will help you achieve these goals, develop healthy and effective reading habits, and build strong leadership qualities in yourself and those you mentor.

Instead of "Words, words," you can reply, "Though this be madness, yet there is method in [i]t."[2] This is the first step to reading like a top leader.

Words, Words

This book teaches you to read like a leader. You will learn the difference between how most people read and how top leaders approach books. In the process, you will have the opportunity to develop the skills of reading like a leader. This will have a huge impact on your life, career, and leadership abilities.

Many years ago, Mortimer Adler, the editor of *The Great Books of the Western World*, wrote a book entitled *How to Read a Book*. The focus of this book was learning to read less like a student and more like a scholar. Later, Yale literary expert Harold Bloom wrote *How to Read a Book and Why*, which taught readers to read more creatively and with a less rote approach. Neither of these books focused on how to read like a leader, however. Yet reading like a leader is vitally important.

In short, leaders read differently.

Sensus Plenior

But what exactly is the difference? Bestselling author Oliver DeMille described leadership reading with the Latin term *sensus plenior*. This is the opposite of *sensus solum*, which literally means "dry land" or, in other words, to read in search of one meaning or to find the one right answer. In contrast, *sensus plenior* means to read the full meaning or even to find multiple meanings. Those who read this way read in search of ideas, thoughts, inspiration, and direction.

This is how top leaders read. Instead of being limited to the thoughts of the author, leaders use the words of a book as a starting point, as one input to help them spark creative and new ideas.

This is easier said than done, especially for people who were trained to read in modern schools with an emphasis on finding the "right" answer. Reading to create, think deeply, spark new thoughts, and lead is seldom taught today.

This book is an antidote to the modern way of reading like followers (or not reading at all). It introduces a number of skills that will help you read like a leader. Each skill is immensely helpful, and together, they can help teach you to *think* like top leaders as well.

Overall, this book will teach you how to put "follower" and even "academic" reading behind you and instead read like top leaders. This is a major step toward improving your leadership skills and life success.

Don't Be a Catherine

For example, the way the character Catherine Morland reads in the book *Northanger Abbey*[3] simply isn't enough to make you a leader. She reads purely for entertainment, and as often happens in such cases, she sacrifices real quality for simple or easy amusement. She doesn't think or question as she reads. She just believes everything and lets someone else shape her mind, without even taking care about *who* she allows to have such control over her thinking. In the end, she has brought herself so much trouble with her terrible reading habits that she decides to give up reading altogether.

> True leadership is not achieved by wrapping your mind (and your future) in a box and handing it to whichever stranger happens to walk past.

True leadership is not achieved by wrapping your mind (and your future) in a box and handing it to whichever stranger happens to walk past. Rather than improving your situation, this kind of reading will probably do the opposite. To put it bluntly, this is a *bad* way to read.

We Need Readers Who Are Leaders

We don't need you to read like Miss Morland, and doing so will not help you achieve the leadership results you're hoping for.

In contrast, top leaders learn to read more like the protagonist in Owen Wister's novel *The Virginian*. This cowboy is a true leader in his community, a Rascal, as bestselling author Chris Brady would say. And the way he reads helps him in this role.

The Virginian (as he's commonly known) understands and exemplifies the importance of leadership, and throughout the book, he comes to recognize the power of reading. He travels from town to town and influences both his friends and people he never even meets.

In this way, because of talent, personality, ability, and the needs of the people around him, he is called upon to be a leader.

He takes control of the situation and makes his influence a completely positive one by reading the great books (and discarding the ones that didn't help him with his own life mission), really thinking about them, discussing them deeply with mentors and colleagues, finding the real-life applications that improve his character and leadership abilities, and then implementing them.

This pattern is repeated in many books, from novels like *The Walking Drum* and *Bendigo Shafter*, to business bestsellers like *The One Minute Manager* and *LeaderShift*. Reading the right way matters.

Leadership reading is about taking responsibility for your leadership roles and preparing yourself to meet them well.

In short, top leaders don't read by accident, and they don't suddenly learn something important by accident. They don't read like students, like scholars, or just for entertainment.

They read on purpose, with specific goals in mind, and as a result, they consistently improve as leaders. Helping you become this kind of reader is what this book is all about.

Read on!

> Leadership reading is about taking responsibility for your leadership roles and preparing yourself to meet them well.

PART I
Reading Is Action

*The most successful CEOs are reported to read an average of 60
books and attend more than six conferences a year—whereas the
average American worker reads an average of less than one book
and makes 319 times less income.*

*Although the media often discusses the disparity between the
rich and the poor, they frequently fail to cover the amount of time
and energy the wealthy have committed to reading, studying, and
educating themselves. . . .*

*The most successful people I know read everything they can
get their hands on. They approach a $30 book as though it has
the potential to make them a million dollars. They see every
opportunity to train and educate themselves as the most solid and
sure investment they can make.*

—Grant Cardone
New York Times Bestselling Author[4]

1

WRITE IN YOUR BOOKS

Reading without reflecting is like eating without digesting.
—Edmund Burke

One of the most fundamental and important techniques of great leadership reading is a fantastic technology known as the pen. It is amazing what this one little device (assuming you actually use it) can do for a reader's learning and success. In fact, using it just once through a book can have a lasting impact on generations of potential readers—anyone who comes along later and reads the marked-up book. That's right! Write in your books. All of them!

Your learning and growth—and therefore your success—are greatly increased when you are accompanied by an active pen. This is a key aspect of leadership reading because as you take note of the important things you are learning, you increase your own level of understanding and lay the groundwork

> As you take note of the important things you are learning, you increase your own level of understanding and lay the groundwork for future readers.

for future readers (including yourself, when you reread the written-in book) to read at higher levels.

Creative Reading

Ralph Waldo Emerson once said, "One must be an inventor to read well. There is then creative reading as well as creative writing." This is crucially important. It means readers should have their thinking caps on as they read so their learning isn't limited to the words and thoughts of the author. But while they have their thinking caps *on*, they need to remember to keep their pen caps *off*. By doing so, they are in a sense combining both creative reading and creative writing. By making reading an *active* process, instead of employing the usual *passive* method, readers can exponentially increase the effectiveness of their reading, thinking, and leadership skills.

Marked-Up Books Are More Valuable

Many top leaders, now and in history, even go out of their way to purchase used books with notes from various previous readers so they can add to the number of minds and voices directly involved in their conversation with themselves and the author. Having notes from five mentors in one book is obviously better than having notes from only one.

For example, successful business leader Orrin Woodward is known for spending hours in used-book stores searching out the right books to read. People who have visited him at his home have often found themselves at one of the local stores perusing various works—many of them marked up with the notes of earlier readers.

Frankly, it doesn't even matter who wrote the notes in the books you read! Having a variety of worldviews, experiences, and opinions interacting and debating over a shared experience (the author's text) opens all kinds of doors in a reader's brain and helps him or her truly optimize the reading experience.

Write in Red!

By the way, these notes shouldn't just be positive or approving. Readers often learn the most from content they read that they absolutely hate or disagree with. Notes should include underlined or highlighted passages, references to other relevant books, angry arguments, or point-by-point proofs of why the author (or a past reader) is wrong or right. They should also include epiphanies, paraphrases, and so forth. Sometimes readers will comment on a note they made themselves in a past reading or on one made by some other reader. This is truly *active* reading.

> Saving your precious thoughts in writing makes them more accessible to you when you want to find them again in the future.

This level of reading engages real thinking and takes the reader deeply into the material of the book. This is leadership reading.

Another reason this is so vital to leadership reading is that recording and thereby saving your precious thoughts in writing makes them more accessible to you when you want to find them again in the future. For example, one of the most famous works by John Adams, *Discourses on Davila*, was taken primarily from notes he had kept in his books. Because he kept track of so many of his important thoughts, questions, and epiphanies as he was reading, he was able

> Sometimes leaders get the inspiration they need to deal with problems or questions in their lives long before the issues arise; writing those answers down helps leaders preserve them for the moment they're really needed.

to use them when he needed to in his leadership career. He turned many of his marginal notes into articles, speeches, and books.

Sometimes leaders get the inspiration they need to deal with problems or questions in their lives long before the issues arise; writing those answers down helps leaders preserve them for the moment they're really needed.

"Wow!"

To summarize, write in your books! Don't write in other people's books, but do write in yours. Write in the margins. Write things like "Wow!"; "I disagree"; "!"; "?"; "So true!"; etc. Write whole sentences or just a word or two. Underline key sentences and circle great passages. Also take notes in the blank pages at the front and back of each book.

In the words of business leader Chris Brady: "As you read, use notations, stars, smiles, exclamation points, etc. When you finish a book, go back and read your own highlights and underlines before putting the book on the shelf. Discuss what you've read with someone soon after reading it, and apply what you've read to something in your life immediately."

Brady also teaches that an important aspect of writing in your books, thus increasing their value and future usability, is to create an outline of the book in the pages at the back of the book and keep a list of new vocabulary words in the front.

What a great idea! By doing this, you'll be making it much easier to find important concepts and ideas when you need them, and you'll also be keeping track of new words you want to learn.

By writing the new words in the front of the book, you'll ensure that you learn several valuable lessons from the book *this* time through. And by making a good outline in the back, you'll be able to learn and find important information anytime you need, without having to read the entire book again. Note that increased vocabulary often coincides with better leadership abilities.

Some people prefer to keep the pages of their books clean and instead take notes in a notebook. However, this practice is not nearly as effective. While writing in a notebook does achieve the more active level of reading for *the current time* through the book, it is considerably less permanent and loses the impact on rereadings and future readers. Top leaders more often write directly in the book! By writing their notes on the actual pages of the book, top leaders can ensure that every time they or others read the book, they will be enriched at a higher level than if they read only the author's text.

Add Value

The many non-leader–oriented systems of reading we often see have taught us that any markings in a book decrease its value, but leaders understand that when it comes to ideas in books, the more the merrier.

If the goal of owning a book is just to put it on a shelf and admire its shininess, it's probably better if no one has ever touched, read, or written in it. It's a decoration and not really a book at all.

If, on the other hand, the goal is to read it, learn from it, and benefit from having done so by becoming a better leader, writing your valuable thoughts in it, and encouraging anyone else who reads it to do the same, will actually increase its value exponentially.

Of course, it's important to note that the rules are a little bit different if you're reading a book that isn't yours. We aren't suggesting that you write in borrowed books, library books, or the books you skim through during bookstore perusals. Not at all! Real leaders recognize the importance of respecting the property of others, and they take care to return borrowed items in good condition.

Your friends may enjoy adding your notes to the collection in their books, or they may not, so don't mark them up without permission. In this case, it's okay to use a notebook on the side to capture your ideas and insights, but be sure to put them in a place where they won't be forgotten or lost—and where you can review them the next time you read the same book.

If you can find a way to *own* the books you're reading and really mark them up with notes, you will get more out of them, especially over time, than if you have to rely on someone else's collection to have the book you need when you need it—especially since your notes will be floating around in a notebook somewhere rather than on the pages of the book itself. Sometimes borrowing books works out just fine, and you don't have any problems. But other times, it can mean you have to start at ground zero when you go to reread the book or find important quotations or passages later on.

For all these reasons, it's a good idea to purchase rather than borrow your books whenever economically possible. And in fact, as we'll discuss in depth throughout this book, now is a great time to start building your own personal library.

Get Involved

Active readership is a vital step toward becoming a leadership reader. Readers are protégés, and authors are mentors. As with any great mentor, authors and books don't have the power to completely transform their readers without a little help. Protégés will only truly excel if they're willing to do their part and take *action*.

Writing your notes in your books is a powerful way to act. So if you don't have a pen handy right now, this is a perfect time to take a break and go get one. You will get way more out of your reading if you approach it actively, thinking and discussing with the text, the author, and yourself by writing as you read.

> Active readership is a vital step toward becoming a leadership reader.

Most of the mainstream eReaders out there even allow you to insert notes as you read.

Take action! Write in your books. As you do, you will greatly improve both your leadership reading and your leadership skills.

2

START WITH A QUESTION

*Which would you rather be if you had the
choice—divinely beautiful or dazzlingly
clever or angelically good?"*
—L. M. Montgomery

One of the most important aspects of leadership reading is asking the right questions, in particular, approaching every book and other reading with targeted and focused questions. Readers who wait for the book to tell them what it's about are missing an enormous opportunity.

Top leaders understand that books should be used to their advantage, to help them accomplish their personal goals, solve their actual problems, and answer their most pressing questions. Rather than working for the book, following its lead, or letting it define the lessons they learn, leadership readers let the book work for *them*, follow *their* lead, and help *them* achieve *their* predefined objectives.

> Readers who wait for the book to tell them what it's about are missing an enormous opportunity.

This is most effective when readers compile a list of questions before reading a book. These questions can be specific to the book, but they are even more helpful when they address the most important challenges readers are currently facing in their life, career, family, and business.

Having specific questions already written down when you open a book to read it achieves at least two important things:

1. It focuses your subconscious mind on the task of finding answers to those questions, thus bringing a higher rate of targeted inspiration and creativity. The subconscious is much bigger than the conscious, and choosing to harness its power to solve problems is a tremendous asset.

2. It helps you read with express intent, and by defining your purpose, you are able to both direct your work toward it and gauge your effectiveness and success.

Think Broadly

In short, readers should prepare a list of questions based on current needs and then read books looking for answers and guidance. The questions will sometimes be obviously connected to the subject of the book. For example, you may look for advice on marriage or parenting in *The 5 Love Languages*[5] or *The Anatomy of Peace*.[6] Other times, the questions might seem to have nothing to do with the book, like questions on how to improve public speaking while reading *A Month of Italy* by Chris Brady.

Leaders understand that important answers often come from unexpected places, so they don't limit themselves to getting business advice *only* from business books, mentoring advice *only* from books on mentoring, and so forth. Because much of the learning derived from any book comes from the reader's own thoughts, it isn't always necessary to stay "on topic."

> Leaders understand that important answers often come from unexpected places.

Mind Your Own Thoughts

Minding your own thoughts is very important. In our modern conveyor-belt education system,[7] most of us have been taught to focus on the words of the author.

In contrast, top leaders know that the most important ideas that come as they read are from their own thoughts. These leaders know what challenges their businesses are facing and what those they lead really need. As they read, then, the book will spark thoughts about these issues. Indeed, answering questions that benefit others is the most important reason to read.

Reading a variety of books to answer big questions helps readers receive fuller and deeper answers, and reading to answer specific questions allows them to learn expressly needed lessons and achieve success in particular areas.

Workshop

1. What are your top five leadership and business challenges right now?

_____

_____

_____

_____

_____

2. What are your top five personal, family, and life challenges right now?

_____

_____

_____

_____

_____

From now on, whenever you read a book, article, or blog or listen to an audio, keep an open mind and consciously watch to see if any ideas or answers to these challenges come to you. Take an active role in seeking such answers. In fact, *expect* such answers to come, and pay close attention. You'll almost certainly be surprised by the excellent ideas you not only read and hear but also generate. And when they come, write them down!

3

BEGIN WITH A PLAN

By failing to prepare, you are preparing to fail.
—Benjamin Franklin

Leaders start with a plan. When they sit down to read a book, aside from knowing what questions they need answered, they also know where they're coming from in life and where they hope to go. They write their strengths and their weaknesses so they can learn ways to turn the weaknesses into strengths and build on the strengths they already have.

By having a clear idea of where they are, leadership readers are better able to target where they want to go and what goals they plan to achieve. They can more easily recognize principles and lessons that apply directly to their own personal needs.

As J. R. R. Tolkien wrote in *The Hobbit*, "It does not do to leave a live dragon out of your calculations, if you live near him." Leaders understand that by including any issues and life goals (live dragons) in their calculations, they're actually setting themselves up for even greater success by preparing for likely challenges and providing accordingly.

> By having a clear idea of where they are, leadership readers are better able to target where they want to go and what goals they plan to achieve.

Leaders also learn and benefit immensely from considering the strengths and weaknesses of their partners, colleagues, and mentees before and as they read. Doing so helps them receive valuable inspiration and insight into those relationships, which leads to more effective mentoring and leadership.

Plan for You and Others

Once they have an outline of their own strengths and goals as well as those of their colleagues and protégés, top leaders have an excellent beginning plan for what they want to learn about as they read. In addition to these strengths and goals, leaders also consider their greatest needs and overarching challenges (which are different from needs). Again, by doing this, leaders are preparing to have increasingly effective and relevant reading experiences.

Prepare for Later

Another thing leaders do as they apply the principles of starting with a plan, beginning with a question, and writing in their books is lay the groundwork for future speeches, articles, books, and influence. When readers go through books looking for inspiration and information to include in future speaking, writing, or leadership, they are almost certain to find plenty of ideas.

Applying these techniques helps them take advantage of these opportunities, optimizing their reading and its impact on their leadership.

The following exchange from *Alice's Adventures in Wonderland* expresses this point in a potent way:

> "Would you tell me, please, which way I ought to go from here?"
>
> "That depends a good deal on where you want to get to," said the Cat.
>
> "I don't much care where—" said Alice.

"Then it doesn't much matter which way you go," said the Cat.

"—so long as I get SOMEWHERE," Alice added as an explanation.

"Oh, you're sure to do that," said the Cat, "if you only walk long enough."[8]

The Cat explained to Alice that every path leads somewhere, eventually, but if you don't have a specific destination in mind, then any old path will do. This is also true in reading. If you just read a book without particular questions or goals, who knows what you'll get? But if you read with specific leadership concerns in mind, the reading will almost always directly improve your leadership ability and wisdom.

> If you read with specific leadership concerns in mind, the reading will almost always directly improve your leadership ability and wisdom.

Know Where You're Going

Laurence J. Peter added to this conversation when he said, "If you don't know where you are going, you will probably end up somewhere else."[9] This implies that those who don't make a special effort to be where they want to be will end up somewhere drastically less pleasant. Again, this is true in reading a book.

In fact, as many leaders have observed, if you don't know where you're going, there's a good chance *you're already there.* People who aren't actively pursuing a clearly defined vision have likely pretty much peaked in their journey for success—unless they get a new vision and goal at some point.

Leaders understand that it *does* matter where they end up, and they also know that they are ultimately responsible for getting themselves there. To accomplish this, they need a vision and an effective plan of action.

In short, top leaders start reading with a plan. They write their strengths and motivations along with those of their colleagues and mentees. They write their needs and challenges as well as their goals and major concerns. This becomes the outline of what they want to learn about as they read. And in writing it, they help prepare themselves for future influence in many other ways and areas of life.

When you sit down to read (or listen to an audio or attend an event) with a list of key questions, strengths, and leadership challenges, you are reading (or listening) like a top leader—and the results are often amazing.

4

Be Open

A mind is like a parachute.
It doesn't work if it is not open.
—Frank Zappa

As we said in the last two chapters, leaders understand the importance of vision and planning in achieving their goals. They know the importance of "beginning with the end in mind," as Stephen Covey put it.

They have a written list of what they need and want, and when they read, they use this list to seek valuable insight from each book they open. They have a general outline of what they intend to learn about and some specific questions they want to answer. All of this should mostly happen *before* they open the book.

Once these preparations have been made and readers have taken responsibility for choosing the right path to achieve their desired results, it's time for them to sit down, pen in hand, and start reading. That's the *science* of leadership reading.

The Art of Reading

This is where things get a little bit more complicated and a lot more exciting. Some people will be tempted to set "bouncers" at the "door" to their brain to kick out any thought that arises while they read that isn't on their list of concerns and questions or any idea that doesn't fit their plan. Worst of all, they may feel compelled to dismiss a thought or impression that comes to mind simply because it has nothing to do with the book. This is absolutely the wrong approach for real leadership reading.

As you read, be open to any new idea that comes along. If the author wrote it, great. Learn from it. You're reading to learn from the wisdom of the author, after all. But, as we said earlier, if the author doesn't say it but it comes to your mind as you read, pay special attention! It may be even more important than what the author wrote because your mind is bringing it up to you. This thought matters. If it's the answer to one of your questions or directly addresses one of the items on your plan, good for you. If it has nothing to do with your plan or your questions but suddenly pops into your head, take advantage of it because sometimes leaders learn most from things they didn't think to plan for. Plan, follow the plan, and be open to tangents that improve the plan.

> Plan, follow the plan, and be open to tangents that improve the plan.

Plan *and* Improvise

In short, leaders start with a plan because that's a fundamental part of leadership; if you don't know where you're going, you shouldn't be leading anybody. But leaders also know that they don't know everything, that there's always more to learn, and that as they learn, they improve their plans and add more questions.

As Orrin Woodward and Chris Brady taught in their book *Launching a Leadership Revolution*, leaders should follow the system they call PDCA: Plan-Do-Check-Adjust. Leaders make good plans and then take action, but they don't assume their original plan was perfect. They constantly check the results their plans bring them, as well as their developing needs, and they make adjustments to their plans as necessary. As George Bernard Shaw said, "Those who cannot change their minds cannot change anything."

By being open to new and unanticipated ideas and direction, leaders keep themselves open to more learning and previously unimagined levels of success.

> The level of ideas and wisdom drastically increases for readers who are open and who have also paid the price to have a tangible plan of what they most want and need to learn.

Make a plan for what you want to get from your reading. Act on your plan. And then be open so you can improve it as experience and more information increase your understanding and wisdom.

In a way, this kind of open reading is what students and many other people do when they read. But the level of ideas and wisdom drastically increases for readers who are open and who have also paid the price to have a tangible plan of what they most want and need to learn. This is how top leaders read.

5

ARGUE WITH
THE AUTHOR

Reading furnishes the mind only with materials of
knowledge; it is thinking that makes what we read ours.
—John Locke

One way top leaders get the most out of what they're reading is by reading with the mind of a "fighter." This doesn't mean they go around picking fights or hitting people with their books. Nor does it mean they go out of their way to misunderstand what the author is saying or refuse to accept any truth they do find. As Søren Kierkegaard said, "There are two ways to be fooled. One is to believe what isn't true; the other is to refuse to believe what is true."

Those who read with the mind of a fighter understand what the author is saying and keep track of what they agree and disagree with.

When they agree, sometimes they emphasize it by underlining, highlighting, or circling great passages, or they write notes in the margins or pages at the back of the book. Doing this helps them learn a lot as they read now, as well as when they reread in the future.

It is even more important, however, to take note of the things they disagree with. Many top leaders will tell you that as long as you are just agreeing with everything the author, mentor, or speaker is saying, you aren't really learning yet. It's when you meet some idea that you *don't* agree with that you're really pushing into the learning zone. If you already agree with what's being said, you've already learned many of the most important lessons from the material. If the author is only saying things you agree with, then you already knew most of them.

> If the author is only saying things you agree with, then you already knew most of them.

The Power of *Why*

In contrast, when you face something you disagree with and force yourself to articulate why, you will:

1. Find that your arguments are weak and that you need to give the question more thought and study;

2. Realize that your original opinion was wrong and that you need to learn from the truth of the author; or

3. Discover that you were right and that you have strengthened your conviction through articulation and argumentation.

In any case, your mind-set and leadership skills will be improved by the trial. This process is important for leaders.

Top leaders understand that the right kind of arguing—the kind that forces them to nail down what they truly believe and defend it with supporting points against an opponent—helps them become better leaders. And, of course, writing these arguments and debates in the books they read is a big part of their success.

Practice Makes Perfect

Simply reading books like *The Communist Manifesto* and mindlessly agreeing with everything won't teach you nearly as much as reading it, analyzing where it contains truth, and otherwise attempting to prove the authors wrong. If you make a focused effort to refute the main points, you'll learn much more, your ability to think and reason will be greatly improved, your beliefs in free enterprise will be strengthened and solidified, and you will become a better thinker, reader, speaker, mentor, and leader.

Do versus Know

There is also another kind of disagreeing that is very important. Sometimes people read something and think, "I totally agree with that," but although they mentally accept the point, their actions actually disagree with it. For example, if they read in the book *Financial Fitness*[10] about the importance of saving a percentage of every paycheck they ever receive and say they completely agree with this point but don't actually follow it, they are in disagreement with the book.

> Sometimes people read something and think, "I totally agree with that," but although they mentally accept the point, their actions actually disagree with it.

Again, disagreement is where the most learning occurs. This is true when you mentally disagree with an idea you read and also when your actions aren't aligned with an important point in a book.

In both cases, circle the things you disagree with and write comments in the margins, such as "I disagree! The author is wrong" or "I agree. But I need to actually live this—to do it, starting right now, no excuses!"

Ultimately, the only way to improve some skills is to start *doing* them. Sitting around thinking about what you hope to be good at is not going to get you there. To achieve the results you want, you must take action. Similarly, simply letting the book speak to you is not going to make you a better leader unless you apply what you've learned.

Creating an argument between you and the author that requires you to take initiative, critically analyze the situation, pinpoint areas of weakness, think creatively, innovate, improve upon what the author says, and solve problems will make you a better leader because it takes you through the leadership process and gives you leadership experience and practice.

> To achieve the results you want, you must take action.

Use Both Types of Disagreement

Note that these two kinds of disagreement can be applied together. For example, as you read *The Communist Manifesto*, you might write remarks like the following in the blank pages at the back of the book:

> Marx was wrong mainly because he designed a system that promotes equality by bringing everyone down to the lowest possible level instead of seeking progress by helping people achieve the mind-set that will enable them all to lift themselves from failure to success.
>
> Sometimes I make this same mistake. I need to do less Marxian-style lecturing to my teenage son on obeying my every word and more of teaching him how to make good decisions independent of me.

Both of these are examples of using disagreement with the author to really improve as a leader. Leaders use the process of arguing with the author to show them how to wrestle with other challenges that come their way and win. And by doing this with every book they read, they give themselves training that helps lead to real victories in various facets of life: family, relationships, work, school, career, community, and so on.

Try It in Levels

Many books will teach you so much that you won't feel the need to argue. You'll be so busy writing down the excellent ideas in the book that you won't even think about disagreements. But be sure to take note of ideas you agree with but aren't really living and applying. As we mentioned above, that's actually a disagreement. Until you live it, you don't truly agree with it.

If, however, you find yourself struggling to learn much from a book you are reading, try arguing with the ideas of the author—and write your disagreements. As you think through the concepts, you'll frequently realize the author is right, but the process of thinking everything through is a great teacher. And sometimes you'll gain important insights as you clarify how a book is wrong about something.

> Until you live it, you don't truly agree with it.

Arguing with the author is one of the quickest and most effective ways to make a book more interesting and more helpful. Top leaders use and learn from both methods of disagreeing when they read.

6

ARGUE WITH YOURSELF

Schizophrenia may be a necessary
consequence of literacy.
—Marshall McLuhan

The technique of arguing with yourself is similar to arguing with the author but adds an extra level of depth. This
happens when you reread books that have your old notes
in them.

C. S. Lewis said, "Clearly one must read every good book at
least once every ten years." Leaders
understand that rereading the books
that taught them the most and most
shaped who they are today is an
essential facet of leadership reading.

> One of the most
> interesting and valuable
> experiences in leadership
> reading occurs when you
> find yourself having a
> debate with five different
> readers and every
> one of them is you.

This can be a fun exercise because
as you go along and see past notes and
comments you wrote in a book, you
will see a younger, less experienced
version of yourself. And because
you will have grown so much since that time, you'll probably have
plenty to disagree about—so catalogue it!

One of the most interesting and valuable experiences in
leadership reading occurs when you find yourself having a debate
with five different readers and every one of them is you. This may

seem funny at first, but when you experience it, you'll realize how much you've learned.

Every time you reread a book, try using a new color of pen so you can distinguish your separate voices and track your progress and growth. And then argue with yourself! When you see older notes you now disagree with, explain yourself. Have a debate. Figure out why you've changed your mind. This is a key part of leadership—to understand and learn from your own changes.

Stand Up

As Ben Goldacre said, "You cannot reason people out of a position they did not reason themselves into." Leaders understand the importance of knowing what they believe and especially *why* they believe it. Leaders stand for something! And this often starts with their reading.

Arguing with yourself as you read is an excellent way to test your opinions and beliefs so you're better able to avoid blind spots or false mind-sets. It also helps you clarify who you really are and what you stand for.

As you argue with your current and past selves in books and notes, you increase your ability to think like a top leader. You also raise the value of your books (meaning how much you and others glean from them when you read them). In addition, you now have at your fingertips an excellent account that allows you to check results and development and adjust your plans for future action.

This is the reason aristocratic families in history often passed down collections of books to their posterity. The notes of past leaders make the books incredibly valuable. If you didn't inherit such a library, start the tradition now and pass it on to your posterity. This is a meaningful and powerful way to leave a legacy of leadership and wisdom.

7

Read Several Books at Once

Books to the ceiling,
Books to the sky,
My pile of books is a mile high.
How I love them! How I need them!
I'll have a long beard by the time I read them.
—Arnold Lobel

At this point, you're probably feeling like we've told you to go against every rule you were ever taught about reading. *Exactly!* So write in your books, start with questions, begin with a plan, listen to your thoughts even more than the author's words, be open, argue with the author, really pay attention to the author, and argue with yourself as you read.

In that same spirit, one of the most effective ways to achieve leadership reading is to read several books at a time. So instead of having one book you're in the middle of right now, you should actually have five or six. This is effective for two main reasons.

Read More

First of all, people who have five or six books to choose from every time they think about reading typically read a lot more than those who have only one.

Why? It's quite simple, really. What happens when you're not in the mood to read the book you're in the middle of? Well, sometimes you push yourself through it anyway, but more often, you find something else to do with your time. And often, even if you do decide to push through the book, you do it with so little energy or focus that you really

> People who have five or six books to choose from every time they think about reading typically read a lot more than those who have only one.

don't get much out of it. You forget to apply the other techniques of leadership reading, revert to student reading, and continue on just to finish the book. This is not the way top leaders read.

The bottom line is this: The chances of your being in the mood to read are much higher if you have several books to choose from. Thus, you'll likely read more often, and your reading will be more effective if you're excited and motivated about it.

Sometimes you just don't "feel" a specific book in a given moment, and that's okay. But it shouldn't mean you don't read. If you have numerous other titles to look over when you feel this way, there's a good chance you can follow up with, "I'm not in the mood for that one, but I am in the mood for this one."

While it may take longer to finish reading individual books, the amount of overall reading done in a week, a month, a year, is far higher than if low energy about one book means a break from reading altogether.

Part of this can include having several books and also various audios at once—so if you're not in the mood to read, you can just listen instead.

Think More

Second, since the main point of leadership reading is to think and act on higher levels and to get important answers to questions and challenges you face as a leader, you'll actually get more out of each book by reading others at the same time. In other words, the focus isn't on the book you're reading but on the questions and challenges you're seeking to answer as you read. With this approach, several books are far better than one.

Thinking about something you recently read in Orrin Woodward's *RESOLVED* while also reading *The Weight of Glory* by C. S. Lewis can help you come up with ideas and answers that would never have come if you didn't have the recent connection.

> The focus isn't on the book you're reading but on the questions and challenges you're seeking to answer as you read. With this approach, several books are far better than one.

Writing these thoughts directly in the books will help future readers make important connections and learn powerful truths as well. For example, in the margin of Lewis's book, next to his thoughts about how friendship accounts for maybe half of the happiness in the world, you write, "See Woodward, *RESOLVED*, the chapter on friendship." And since *RESOLVED* is sitting in the stack of books you're reading right now, you can quickly grab it, go to the chapter on friendship, and write in the margin: "Compare this with C. S. Lewis, *The Weight of Glory*, the chapter on the inner ring."

Someday you'll want to give a speech on friendship, and when you turn to the friendship chapter in *RESOLVED* for ideas, you'll have a bunch of notes on the topic in the margins. You'll read references to C. S. Lewis and Aristotle, and your speech will be halfway prepared!

In this way, reading several books at once helps leaders add more voices to their deep and important conversations, much as the notes of previous readers do. In fact, if you bought your copy of

The Weight of Glory at a used-book store and it has a bunch of notes from past readers, you'll have even more resources to help you.

Raise the Bar

In short, the goal is not just to find out what an individual author is saying. The idea is to become a leadership reader by reading to learn things that will improve your ability to be an excellent person and a more effective leader. Thus, the more great books you receive mentorship from, the better. And if you can get them to interact (by reading authors' various books at the same time, making mental connections between important ideas, and then taking notes about them in the books), you're becoming a leadership reader at an even higher level.

> The more great books you receive mentorship from, the better.

So, rather than looking at your library and selecting a single title to work on for a while, pick five or six, or at least three or four, and make a special shelf to keep them on. Put them where you can easily see and access them from your reading spot—next to your desk or your chair or wherever it is that you do most of your reading.

Variety of Styles and Topics

Typically, it's best to select books written in a variety of styles covering an array of topics. Having a wide selection will better achieve both objectives of reading several books at once (keeping you interested in at least one of your books) and helping you make important connections between different authors. For example, Tom and Jillian wanted to join a monthly book club, but they weren't sure whether to subscribe to a general book club or a more targeted business leader book club. They tried one for a time and then the other.

But they had trouble deciding which to stay with because they liked both lists. They struggled with the fact that one had to wait on the other to finish reading before getting the copy of the book, but otherwise, they enjoyed reading the monthly book and discussing it together.

Then a mentor suggested that they subscribe to both. They decided to try it, and they both loved the results. There was always something for each of them to read. And they found that by reading two books every month, they actually learned a lot more from each individual book.

Buckminster Fuller and Stephen Covey call this "synergy," where the whole is greater than the sum of the parts. Tom and Jillian learned more by reading both books in the same month than they did when they read the books in consecutive months. They were able to pull ideas and insights from both books as they focused on their family and business needs and goals. Reading two books during the same month actually created greater depth; they learned more from each book because they compared the two.

> Reading two books during the same month actually created greater depth; they learned more from each book because they compared the two.

One way to find a wide selection of good books to read together is to join a monthly book club or sign up for a monthly book subscription, just like Tom and Jillian did. This can help you find books that would otherwise be unknown to you and help you improve your leadership reading. An easy way to go about this is to go to life-leadership-home.com and look into the subscriptions, such as the LIFE, LLR, and AGO Series. These are all programs that send you a book and some audios every month that are chosen by top leaders who have enough experience to cut past the junk and recommend materials that will really help you. This is also a great way to add variety to your collection.

If applying the techniques of leadership reading to six books in a month seems overwhelming, consider creating a single list of leadership questions that fits all and then making a few unique additions to the list for each particular book. Doing so will keep you focused on reading to achieve leadership, excellence, and success.

Variety of Fun and Challenging Books

When you find yourself avoiding one of the books in your stack, either put it back in your main library to be pulled out at some future date or push yourself to read it. Both can be valuable, and part of leadership reading is deciding when it's right to move on to more exciting projects and when the less engaging books really need your attention.

Some books are hard, and that's something to take into consideration. Hard work isn't good just because it's hard; it's good when and if it achieves important results. But anyone who has achieved such results did so by doing a fair amount of hard work. Top leaders try to consistently make sure their hard work is also smart work. This applies in reading, just as in everything else.

> Hard work isn't good just because it's hard; it's good when and if it achieves important results.

Therefore, have both fun books and more challenging books in your stack of current reading. And when you find a book that's particularly difficult, seek a mentor's advice. Part of growth includes pushing yourself to go outside your comfort zone and do hard things.

Leaders learn that success means taking a "voyage of a Viking," as Tim Marks put it, and choosing to "toughen up," as Claude Hamilton wrote, which both include doing difficult things because they are right and effective. A mentor can help you know the best times and ways to do this.

To sum up, top leaders often read several books at a time. As a result, they nearly always read more over time, and they also consistently get more out of what they read. This is a key technique for successful leadership reading.

PART II
Read the Greats

The story—from Rumpelstiltskin *to* War and Peace—*is one of the basic tools invented . . . for the purpose of understanding. There have been great societies that did not use the wheel, but there have been no societies that did not tell stories.*
—Ursula K. Le Guin

8

READ GREAT BOOKS

*Reading good books ruins you
for enjoying bad books.*
—Mary Ann Shaffer

L eaders have to deal with big challenges, and to do so effectively, they need to have big thoughts and big ideas. In order to train their minds so that big ideas are the norm, leaders have to feed them with the great ideas, great thinkers, and great books of history. By reading the greatest works of humanity, leaders build their repertoire of knowledge in powerful ways.

> In order to train their minds so that big ideas are the norm, leaders have to feed them with the great ideas, great thinkers, and great books of history.

Over the centuries of human existence, leaders have come up with some pretty amazing answers and solutions to their problems. The best leaders know that to really optimize their impact, they need to learn from past leaders' experience by reading great books.

Go Big

By applying the techniques of leadership reading and actively thinking while you read, you can learn great leadership principles and lessons from practically anything, but reading great books improves the process and speeds up success.

Allan Bloom wrote, "The failure to read good books both enfeebles the vision and strengthens our most fatal tendency— the belief that the here and now is all there is."[11] Leaders have to see the world in a "big picture" sort of way if they're going to be truly effective, and reading great books significantly improves this leadership skill. By reading the greatest books, leaders are able to awaken their minds and open their eyes to the real needs of the world, along with the specific important impact each of them can make.

Get a List

Of course, great books can be found in all sorts of places, and the more one reads, the more one develops a taste for excellence and greatness. The best place to start is to get a good mentor who can help you weed out the mediocre and point out the ones that are really worth your time. It's better to learn from the experience of someone who's done what you're hoping to accomplish than to try to experience every possibility yourself. So find a good mentor who can help you locate the best books (many mentors have already printed such lists) and guide you in your leadership reading.

> It's better to learn from the experience of someone who's done what you're hoping to accomplish than to try to experience every possibility yourself.

A top reading list is also presented in later chapters of this book. Now is the time to start reading truly great books—or read even more if you've already begun.

9

KEEP GOOD COMPANY

Outside of a dog, a book is a man's best friend.
Inside of a dog it's too dark to read.
—Groucho Marx

The power of association is real. Jim Rohn said, "You are the average of the five people you spend the most time with." Good leaders understand this principle and make sure to keep good company. They seek their friends among the successful, hardworking, and excellent. If you look at the closest friends of top leaders, you will almost always find that they are also top leaders in some way or another.

This is not a coincidence. Many top leaders make a point of associating with people who will "bring up their average" and help them be better.

Since great leaders are also great readers, they inevitably spend much of their time with books and authors. That said, top leaders take care to choose their books wisely, just as they do their friends. As Geraldine Brooks said, "To know a man's library is, in some measure, to know a man's mind."

> Since great leaders are also great readers, they inevitably spend much of their time with books and authors.

Just as people's habits and character are often shaped by the habits and character they experience most often from their closest friends, their ideas and minds are often shaped by the ideas and minds they experience in their most cherished books.

Those who wish to be truly great leaders should be careful to avoid friends, ideas, and books that are damaging to that end.

Books Are Friends

In his book *Toughen Up!*, business leader Claude Hamilton wrote:

> If you spend your time with people who are willing to give up when things get tough, their attitude will have a tendency to influence your choices. Part of courage is loving yourself enough to say, "I will not allow my goals to be hindered by those who aren't willing to achieve theirs."
>
> There is a reason why so few people make it in Special Forces and only a few make it to the top of business success. Associations matter, and the more we can associate with those who are on the path of success—in whatever they've chosen as their field of focus—the better.[12]

Claude's words apply to books as well as people.

Just Say No

Leaders understand that some books simply aren't worth their time because such books actually lead them *away* from their goals, dreams, and purpose. When this happens, top leaders exert their power as the reader. They recognize that they don't read books simply to finish (as many students are taught to do) but because they hope to achieve certain results, and if a book is dangerous or unhelpful to those results, they put it down and read something else.

Leaders do not allow the compulsion to read like a follower to dictate their success or failure. As a leader (or even as a potential leader), you are the boss of your reading experience. If you stop reading a book, read several at once, write in them, or apply any of the leadership reading techniques, no brother-in-law's rules of "this is how you have to read" are going to stop you. As Elizabeth Bennett puts it in the movie version of *Pride and Prejudice*, "Lady Catherine will never know."[13]

> Leaders do not allow the compulsion to read like a follower to dictate their success or failure.

Lady Catherine was known for butting into other people's business, but the most amazing thing about her hobby of meddling was that most people consistently allowed her nosy interference and actually listened to her intrusive advice.

> You are the boss of your reading experience.

Certainly you should listen to the wisdom of your mentors and others who have set the example of attaining the kinds of goals you are seeking, but too frequently, people are easily swayed by the opinions of those who shouldn't be emulated. To read like a top leader, learn from top leaders—not from the crowd.

Use Judgment

Of course, you should use judgment when deciding whether to stop or continue reading a book; not every hard, depressing, or unexciting book is a bad book. In fact, sometimes they're the ones that teach the most. But using judgment includes realizing that there is a time and a place for either answer.

You may know someone who has a personal policy of finishing every book he or she ever starts, no matter what. Sadly, this mentality is not uncommon, even though it's a terrible policy and can be a colossal waste of time.

Think about it: If you get halfway through the book and realize it's truly worthless, personally unhelpful, or even downright evil, why should you keep reading? The answer is you shouldn't.

This goes back to the idea that hard work isn't good because it's hard; it's good only if and when it accomplishes important things and does so in the best ways. Reading a book, or finishing a book, is not good just because the world needs to have a higher average of books read and finished by you in a year.

On the contrary, reading and finishing books is only good when doing so will actually make a positive difference in your life and leadership. Period. If finishing a book is a waste of time or a danger to your productivity and influence as a leader, then the best leadership reading technique you can apply is the one called "slam it shut and move on with your life."

That said, you have to be honest with yourself and not use this power as a copout or an excuse to avoid hard or difficult readings that will really push you to greater levels of excellence and leadership ability.

Top leaders understand the power of association, and they keep good company—in books as well as people. Read quality, not junk.

10

VARIETY IS THE SPICE

*Only the very weak-minded refuse to be
influenced by literature and poetry.*
—Cassandra Clare

Top leaders value variety. By recognizing the importance of strength in many areas, leaders also accept that truth and valuable lessons can come from various sources and in different ways. Top leaders include an assortment of genres, styles, and topics in their personal readings and libraries.

As we mentioned earlier, great books can come from a variety of places. That said, it's important to find and read great books wherever they may be. Leaders understand that great reading includes great novels, great biographies, great self-help books, great poetry, great histories, great leadership and business books, and so forth. For example, voracious readers like Orrin Woodward, Chris Brady, and Oliver DeMille read approximately six genres at the same time, including business, history, theology, classics, fiction, economics, leadership, and governance.

Again, mentors and leadership reading lists can help you find the best books to read in each of these genres, but the main point is that

> Narrow reading causes shallow leading.

those who are well read in diverse genres and topics will have more influence as mentors, parents, and business leaders and will be better thinkers and problem solvers. Narrow reading causes shallow leading.

By the way, those who read about various subjects in different genres usually enjoy their reading a lot more than people who limit their reading to only one or two topics or styles.

Fun Matters

In the same vein, the road to great leadership is sometimes hard, and at times, it feels very serious and important. But that doesn't mean it has to be *too* serious, and it certainly shouldn't be boring or monotonous.

One of the best parts of leadership reading is that it takes advantage of the things you love and makes them work toward your success. You'll actually learn more if you enjoy most of what you read, so have fun! Reading isn't just about accomplishing big goals or solving big problems, but you can do both even as you're having fun.

Leaders Leading Everywhere

There are great books in every genre, and if you pick the right ones, you can learn important leadership lessons from every field of knowledge. Just apply the techniques of great leadership reading in whatever you read, and over time, read the best books in every genre and style that interests you.

> There are great books in every genre, and if you pick the right ones, you can learn important leadership lessons from every field of knowledge.

Your ideas and epiphanies will usually exhibit more ingenuity and creativity when you're reading from several genres and styles at once, especially if you find a way to make reading fun. Emma Cox told the following story of her experience with Leo Tolstoy's *Anna Karenina:*

It's certainly a tough book to read, and a lot of people don't realize that books like this—the really old ones, and the story books—have huge lessons to teach us as leaders. But luckily, when I read it, I was also in the middle of reading *The Prince* by Niccolò Machiavelli, so I had that fresh in my mind.

Reading Machiavelli obviously gave me a lot to think about as far as what true leadership was, and what type of leader I wanted to be. *The Prince* talks a lot about using fear, force, and manipulation to lead, and I'd always believed that love and service were more effective, not to mention more *right.*

These thoughts and questions were running through my head when I picked up *Anna Karenina.* Now Tolstoy's books are certainly a different genre from Machiavelli's, and like I said, they can be tough to read, so I had been taking it pretty slow.

But this time, when I picked it up to read for a while, I was amazed at how many interesting connections about human nature were flying around in my brain!

Reading the examples of so many failing relationships (and all the details of *why* they were failing) after hearing the advice of Machiavelli on so many political issues, helped me realize how important service-oriented leadership is.

Reading each of these books while thinking of the other painted a pretty clear picture of what selfishness, dishonesty, and vanity *really* accomplish in the world, and it certainly isn't goodness or happiness.

As a leader in my family, my community, and my business, I need to be a person who looks to *serve,* not one who looks to control people and take anything I can get from them.

The things I learned from these books were instrumental in my success as a leader. Time and again, I've come back to these lessons, and asked myself: "What kind of leader are you? Are you here for what's right, or just for what you want?"

I've always thought it interesting the way stories teach us lessons that we often miss in other types of books, and I think as we read stories, we actually learn more than from anything else we read.

> "...stories teach us lessons that we often miss in other types of books."
> —Emma Cox

This particular story helped me in my marriage, and with several of my work associates. I was forced to be more honest and more excellent on a personal level; my influence and effectiveness were also increased.

Now, years later, thinking back on that experience, I realize how bizarrely unconnected those books must seem to most people, and all I can do is smile at how awesome the result of that reading session would have been if I had also been reading Chris Brady's *Rascal.*

Top leaders harness and take advantage of the power of passion, fun, and variety to make themselves even better leaders. This is true in leadership and also in readership. Sometimes it takes strange directions that make little obvious sense, but leaders understand that truth—and the vital lessons and techniques of leadership—can come from many sources. And sometimes, as Winston Churchill said, "A change is as good as a rest."

11

STUDY BOOKS LIKE AN ARTIST

*Art never responds to the wish to make it democratic; it is not
for everybody; it is only for those who are willing to undergo
the effort needed to understand it.*
—Flannery O'Connor

Anyone who studies a painting generally does it differently than one who sits down to study a book. This difference is significant to those who hope to develop the skills and mind-set of a leadership reader. When an artist studies, it's usually less about what the original artist meant and more about what the painting or piece of artwork says.

This can be confusing because so often when we use the word *says*, we mean it in the sense of its synonym *speaks*. In such cases, there really is a right or wrong answer and a particular way that everyone should understand it because it has one specific, correct meaning. This is how most readers understand the word *says*.

What Makes the Difference?

Artists—and top leaders—understand the word *says* differently. They take the word and match it to a different synonym: the word *communicates*. When a person reads looking for what the book communicates, it's not about finding one correct answer; it's about finding the most helpful answers.

As we've said in earlier chapters, it's not about what the author or the painter (or anyone else) learned, felt, heard, or thought. It's all about what you as a leader learn, hear, think, and feel. The question should be: What does the painting or the book teach you?

> It's not about what the author or the painter (or anyone else) learned, felt, heard, or thought. It's all about what you as a leader learn, hear, think, and feel.

This leads to another important point that wasn't covered earlier: Great books can teach us a lot, but only if we learn a lot. Readers who apply this principle will become creative readers who actually produce as they read, instead of just consuming. Their learning is an actual creation.

It Takes a Reader

These readers are producing learning, growth, and increased success. And for top leaders, this happens right as they read.

When we talk about the most experienced and hungry students of art, they are actually called artists, as if by studying art, they themselves are creating something rather than just observing. This is a powerful lesson for leaders to learn and apply. While this may seem obvious, top leaders understand its importance. As Orna Ross said, "It takes a great reader to make a great book."

Reading books the way an artist reads art is one of the most important principles of leadership reading. So read looking for real answers to what the book communicates to your needs and current challenges as a leader. This is how top leaders read!

12

READ ANYWHERE

*I find television very educating. Every time somebody turns
the set on, I go into the other room and read a book.*
—Groucho Marx

One of the things that will almost instantly increase your success as a reader is getting into the habit of carrying at least one book with you wherever you go. Much of your time can be used more productively if you happen to have a book on you when you find yourself doing nothing.

Think about it: How many hours in a week do you spend sitting around being bored, staring at your watch, or, heaven forbid, playing a game of Tetris or Angry Birds on your cell phone? Do you ever find yourself on a bench waiting for the bus, in your car waiting for your spouse or kids, or in a doctor's office or the golf club waiting for someone?

> What if many of these moments weren't wasted time or necessary evils but instead valuable leadership training sessions?

Many of us spend a significant amount of time each week waiting for appointments or someone else to do something.

What if many of these moments weren't wasted time or necessary evils but instead valuable leadership training sessions? For top leaders, they often are. How? They carry a book with them in their purse, pocket, or briefcase (or even on their phone), so they can pull it out and read for five or ten minutes at a time here and there.

Surprise!

Most people would be surprised at how much time they're wasting if they ever tried to read a book using only their random moments of free time because they'd see how much that time is worth and how much they could really do with it. Chris Brady once read Leo Tolstoy's *War and Peace* in its entirety on his cell phone, in just this way, in under three months. Top leaders understand the vital importance of taking control of their time, especially the small chunks of it that are so easily wasted.

> Top leaders understand the vital importance of taking control of their time, especially the small chunks of it that are so easily wasted.

The story is told of a young leadership protégée who talked to her friends about the average number of books the wealthy read each year versus the number the middle and lower classes read. She cited a statistic that said the top 5 percent of wealthiest people in the United States read around sixty books a year, while the other 95 percent read an average of only one.[14]

The immediate response of one man she was talking to was that of course they read so much. After all, those people have lots of free time, while the rest of the people have to work.

> The top 5 percent of wealthiest people in the United States read around sixty books a year, while the other 95 percent read an average of only one.

This answer came as a huge shock to the woman because she had understood the statistic in an entirely different way. She continued the discussion, however, hoping the man had a real point. Finally, after he harped for minutes on how selfish and lazy the wealthy are, she interrupted him with a question.

"How many hours do you work every week?"

"Well, depending on the week, forty to fifty. But I'm on call a lot more often than that, and many weeks, I have to travel, which means I work the whole weekend sometimes."

"Okay, that does take up quite a bit of your time. Let me ask you another question: How do you travel? Do you have to do all the driving, or do you carpool or fly?"

"It includes a lot of foreign stuff, so I generally fly. When we do drive, there's usually another guy there, but sometimes it's just me. Why are you asking all these questions, anyway?"

"Well, it seems like your job includes a ton of built-in reading time, don't you think? You can read on the plane, when your coworker is driving, and even when you're alone, you could try using audio books or something. I just have one more question for you: How much TV do you watch each week?"

At about this point, he gave up the argument—before she could mention statistics about how many of the wealthy tend to work a lot more than forty to fifty hours a week.

You've heard it many times, but it bears repeating: The richest, most successful leaders in the world and throughout history have all had the same number of hours in a day as the rest of us. Most of them had to struggle through jobs and commitments that demanded a big portion of their time. The difference is that these men and women took control of their futures by taking control of their time.

> It's easy to be busy, but it's a little harder to be busy doing the right things. Yet this is exactly what top leaders do.

When you're in charge of every minute of your time, and you use each one to build your present and future success, you will achieve it. It's easy to be busy, but it's a little harder to be busy doing the right things. Yet this is exactly what top leaders do.

When to Just Say No

Now there is at least one more aspect of this principle that will make a big difference in your success. Aside from taking advantage of the minutes most people fill with nothing but boredom, top leaders also learn to say no to inferior activities—in favor of a good book.

Maureen Corrigan wrote, "It's not that I don't like people. It's just that when I'm in the company of others—even my nearest and dearest—there always comes a moment when I'd rather be reading a book." Top leaders have to learn when to follow that urge and make it happen.

> Aside from taking advantage of the minutes most people fill with nothing but boredom, top leaders also learn to say no to inferior activities—in favor of a good book.

Of course, this isn't a suggestion that you should burn all your relationship bridges or make all your family and friends hate you by reading books when you should be doing other things. Naturally, leaders understand the necessity of giving real time and energy to the important relationships in their lives. However, they also know that not every option or activity should be a higher priority than reading. Sometimes it's appropriate and right for you to read during or instead of certain other activities.

Here are some ideas on where and when you should be reading, according to top leader Chris Brady:

WHERE Should You Read?

1. Everywhere!

2. Whenever and wherever you travel

3. At the office, when you're on breaks

4. At home

5. In your car (when you're stranded, waiting for someone, etc.)

6. On errands (when you're waiting in line, etc.)

7. In bed

8. In the bathroom

WHEN Should You Read?

1. Always!

2. In little snippets

3. In concentrated moments of time (longer and more focused)

4. On sabbaticals

5. On specific "reading days"

6. During family reading times (Sunday afternoon for two hours, etc.)

That's a lot of great reading! Perhaps instead of "Read Anywhere," this chapter should have been titled "Read *Everywhere*" because that's what many top leaders do. You will be amazed at how far fifteen minutes (or even two or three) here and there will get you when you get into the habit of reading anywhere, anytime—or even better, everywhere, much of the time. And since you are marking up the books as you go, you can start and stop a lot and still maintain your flow of learning.

You will be busy much of your life, but so is everyone who makes a real difference in the world and achieves true success. One thing that sets them apart is that they find time for reading and value their success enough to read when it counts.

13

MAKE AND GROW YOUR LIST

My reading list grows exponentially. Every time I read a book,
it'll mention three other books I feel I have to read. It's like a
particularly relentless series of pop-up ads.
—A. J. Jacobs

As you go about your life, you'll hear about dozens and dozens of books that you ought to read. Not every single one should be your first priority, but they might be important to you during future challenges and opportunities. So, guided by a mentor, build yourself a list.

It's important to remember that this list should *not* be scattered throughout a dozen random notebooks that you'll never look at again. You should have your leadership reading list in a specific place so you can always find it when you need it. This isn't just a bunch of tiny lists, but your *official* list.

The more you read, the more you'll add and remove, but having it will help you when you're stuck between books or finished with one.

As you set goals in conjunction with your list, you'll be able to measure your progress and gauge your success.

Intentional Direction

It will also help you set a direction for your growth and personal improvement, so that you'll be living consciously and with intention. As you set goals in conjunction with your list, you'll be able to measure your progress and gauge your success. Jean de La Fontaine said, "One of the secrets of getting more done is to make a to-do list every day, keep it visible, and use it as a guide to action as you go through the day." In fact, this is one of the oldest leadership skills of all. But when it's applied to reading, it takes on a new light.

People who think it's important to read books (and those who hope to be top leaders should) take advantage of this idea and use it to increase their level of productivity in reading, just as they do with other areas of life.

Keep Tabs on Yourself

By making a list and having it there to look at, you significantly increase the likelihood of actually reading the books on it.

> By making a list and having it there to look at, you significantly increase the likelihood of actually reading the books on it.

It's a good idea to pick the top several titles on your list, along with one that's just really fun for you at the time, and use those as your books to keep near your reading spot. Rather than displaying the whole list, as you would with a daily to-do list, put those top six in a place where you'll see them, and make a point of reading in at least one of them for a minimum of fifteen minutes every day. Then, as you finish each title, get out your list, mark it off in the way that is most fulfilling to you, and pull out the next book to add to your stack. For example, Chris Brady keeps a special journal where he's kept track of every book he's read for the last twenty years! He records the title, the author, and the date he finished the book.

This is helpful for a number of reasons. For one, it keeps you from telling yourself that you're reading a lot when you aren't.

Sometimes this kick in the pants is exactly what you'll need to get yourself moving again after too many long breaks.

One of the most dangerous obstacles to effective and targeted action is the belief that it's happening when it really isn't. Often, we believe we're doing everything we mean to be doing, or that we're really on the right track, when we're really doing a whole lot of nothing.

This method of looking at your goals and plans and keeping a solid record of your actual results is a great way to keep yourself moving in the right direction, instead of allowing yourself to be caught up in the inactivity of self-deception. Orrin Woodward calls this "keeping score" in his book *RESOLVED*. On top of that, you're also keeping an excellent record of your self-directed education, which is a great legacy for later protégés and followers to duplicate and emulate.

All in all, by doing this, you will be constantly reminding yourself of what you want to accomplish in the long run. You will also recognize the things you're accomplishing on a daily and weekly basis. When you give yourself recognition and rewards for each goal you meet, you'll be more excited and motivated to achieve the next one. In this way, making and growing a leadership reading list helps leaders keep track of the big picture, while still advancing in meaningful ways and winning the little battles that will bring larger victories.

14

GET TO KNOW YOUR BOOKS

How do you press a wildflower into the pages of an e-book?
—Lewis Buzbee

One way to increase the impact of your books is to take a few steps to really get to know them before you dive in. This may sound strange, but it really makes a difference for several reasons.

Motivational Factor

One main reason is excitement, or the "motivational factor." How many times have you gone to see a movie because you first saw a preview that got you excited? That's why moviemakers spend so much time and money creating previews and putting them in front of potential movie watchers. Giving yourself a good preview to pique your interest in something you think you should be interested in reading is a very important aspect of leadership and leadership reading.

> Giving yourself a good preview to pique your interest in something you think you should be interested in reading is a very important aspect of leadership and leadership reading.

Getting to know your books is a great way to motivate yourself to actually read them! People who think they don't need motivation—or that motivation is beneath them—are simply missing the point. There never comes a time in a leader's journey when he or she stops needing motivation. As leader and businessman Steve Morgan said, "Motivation is like a shower; if you go a few days without it, you start to stink." Top leaders know that they won't ever stop needing motivation. In fact, realizing just how much they do need it gives leaders real power to grow and lead because it puts them in a position to take responsibility for always having it.

Testing Factor

A second reason for previewing or getting to know your books is the "testing factor." A quick perusal of unfamiliar books is a great way to judge their value and decide whether to read them. There are thousands of books out there, and quite frankly, they're not all worth your time. Sometimes a quick skimming is all they really deserve from you and all you really need from them. Learning to effectively test books at the library or bookstore before you invest in them will save you lots of time and money, enabling you to focus on the books that will really help you become a more effective leader.

Francis Bacon said, "Some books should be tasted, some devoured, but only a few should be chewed and digested thoroughly." It's your responsibility, with the help and advice of mentors, to decide which of these categories each book fits into, and getting to know a book before you actually read the whole thing is an excellent way to make that assessment.

A great example of this is found in the 2003 film *Alex and Emma*. At one point, the two title characters have an argument on the merit of reading the last page of a book in order to decide whether to read the rest. Alex is a novelist, so he believes that reading the last page of a book before you know the whole story is nothing short of literary heresy. Emma, on the other hand, contends that when she sees titles or authors she's never heard of, she has to put them through this test because she wouldn't want to waste her time and energy getting emotionally involved with characters or stories that really aren't worth it.

Now when dealing with tried-and-true books recommended by trustworthy mentors, it's certainly fine to read them in the "right" order, as long as you recognize the value of deciding what you do or do not read.

For top leaders, Emma absolutely wins this debate because, far from being blasphemous, perusing a book before committing to it is a great technique of leadership reading. Skim through potential books, read the table of contents, randomly read a paragraph here and there, and get a feel for what the book will give you. Reading the introduction is often the best test. This actually helps you learn better when you do end up reading the book closely because your memory will tie in this perusal with later reading.

Bestselling business author Marcus Buckingham tells how he did well at Cambridge by studying the table of contents, the first and last chapters, and then skimming the main points of books. Many students who read the books from the first word to the last—without giving their brain this overall tour of the book before reading—did much worse. The difference was that he really focused on *learning* the key points of the reading, not just getting through it.

Depth Factor

A third reason for this kind of introduction is the "depth factor." When you've taken time to really make friends with a book before you learn every detail of its contents, you are able to connect with greater depth than if you simply go blundering in without even a smile. This is the part that sounds weirdest to those of us who were raised as follower readers in school, but top leaders understand the truth of this principle.

When you have a relationship with your book, you learn more, grow more, and change more through the reading, which means the experience is worth more. Just like reading multiple books at once, writing in your books, or rereading past books, having a solid introduction to new books before you read them can help you get more voices involved in the conversation, which increases learning and progress.

> When you've taken time to really make friends with a book before you learn every detail of its contents, you are able to connect with greater depth than if you simply go blundering in without even a smile.

How?

Now that we understand why it's helpful to get to know our books, let's talk about how to actually go about it. Just as there are many reasons for doing it, there are also multiple ways to do it. Ultimately, every leader will develop his or her own method of getting acquainted with a new book before reading. That said, here are a few suggestions that will help you get started and develop your own routine of pre-reading initiation.

Skim the Book

Flip through the pages and read a sentence here and there that sticks out to you. If you own the book, it's a good idea to make notes even in this preliminary stage of reading. Read through some of the headers, callouts, or quotes in the book.

Aside from helping you get to know the book and get excited about reading it, previewing this way takes you to a whole new level of creative reading, so be sure to take lots of notes.

Often, when you do read through the entire book, you'll find

> In this way, you're reading two great books at the same time: the one the author wrote and the one you're writing yourself in your mind (and in the margins).

that your initial perception of what it was about was way off. Yet rather than being unhelpful, that actually makes the whole process even better. Reading headers, quotations, and snippets and letting your mind come up with its own interpretation of what truths they teach can bring you all sorts of fantastic ideas and epiphanies that never occurred to the author. In this way, you're reading two great books at the same time: the one the author wrote and the one you're writing yourself in your mind (and in the margins).

Outline

Chris Brady recommends making an outline of the book in the back pages, as authors used to do in their introductions.[15] This will help you organize the book and get a feel for what you'll be reading and when. It will also be extremely helpful in increasing your retention and your ability to find important ideas years later.

You'll probably add to this and make minor changes as you read the book more deeply, but outlining from the start will help you get a picture of what the book has to say.

Read the Last Chapter

This technique is pretty self-explanatory; just make sure you consider it. Of course, we're not saying that you have to do this with every book you ever read. You're the boss of your reading, so if you agree with Alex and think this is blasphemous, feel free to discard it in your own routine. But it can help you maximize your reading experience and your time. In other words, it's an option, and often, it's a good one.

Multisensory

Something that will help you increase the depth of your relationship with your books, and therefore the depth of your learning, is greeting them with more than just one sense. What this means is that rather just looking at your book, you feel it, hear it, and smell it. Just spend a few minutes running your fingers through the pages. Learn the smell of your book. Read a few selections out loud so you can hear the flow of the words and the style of the writing.

While this seems strange to the inexperienced reader, it actually plays a significant role in your learning and reading process. Top leaders do it all the time. It will advance your relationship with the book to a deeper intimacy.

> Read a few selections out loud so you can hear the flow of the words and the style of the writing.

Going through this multisensory introduction activates your whole brain to the process and takes you out of the habitual approach of the follower reader that basically says, "Open book; turn off brain; read, read, read."

So even if you feel silly, do it! It will improve your reading immensely and make you a better leader.

Personalize

Of course, there are many other ways to get to know your books, and you'll naturally come up with many of your own as you develop as a leadership reader. These few are a great start.

We're not suggesting that all of these are "must do's," but they're all good options. So figure out what's best for you, and realize that it will likely be different for different books and at different times in your life.

Still, using these techniques in whatever configuration works best for you will strengthen your ability to motivate yourself to read great books in a deep and meaningful way while allowing you to more easily sort out the ones that aren't really worth your time. It will also increase how much you learn from every book you read.

15

BOOKSTORE PERUSALS

People can lose their lives in libraries.
They ought to be warned.
—Saul Bellow

As we mentioned earlier, top leaders can often be found lurking in obscure corners of bookstores, looking for the right book. Other times, you'll see them sitting at a table with a stack of twenty books on it and another stack of four or five next to that. In their hands, they'll be holding what you can only assume is the fifth or sixth book of the day.

But did they really read the four or five books next to the big stack while they were sitting in that chair at the bookstore?

The answer to this question is generally unclear to most of us. Today is our lucky day, however, because we're about to learn what these bookstore trips are all about.

The fact is many top leaders go to bookstores to associate with books.

> Many top leaders go to bookstores to associate with books.

Some of them did skim or even read the four or five books in the smaller stack, but only if the books were good ones. If they weren't good, they were discarded without a second thought because top leaders don't waste their time or risk their minds on things that won't bring them closer to success and excellence. A great technique of leadership reading is the bookstore perusal, and this is how it works.

Step 1: Choose Thirty

Go through the bookstore (or library) and start perusing books. Maybe you start with the *New York Times* bestsellers, the self-help section, or the local authors section. Wherever you start, go through the store and build yourself a stack of thirty or so titles that look intriguing to you.

Again, pick titles from assorted genres and authors. The variety will improve your thinking. By reading broadly, you improve your ability to make valuable connections between various aspects of life. This is a vital leadership skill. Sadly, these days, we're often taught that studying broadly makes one a "jack of all trades" and that specialization is the only way to achieve real depth. However, to be able to influence and relate to people from all walks of life, as leaders must do, you have to have both depth and breadth.

> By reading broadly, you improve your ability to make valuable connections between various aspects of life.

Therefore, when you're in the bookstore or library perusing things to read that will increase your leadership effectiveness or address specific goals, remember that variety and breadth will make you even better at what you do!

Step 2: Go at It!

Once you have your thirty titles in a stack next to a comfy chair, it's time to start perusing individual books. Just pick one up and start getting to know it. Have fun with it! If a book isn't meeting your standards, put it in a reject stack and pick up the next one.

You may end up reading several chapters of a book. Great! Learn from it. You may find a few you want to buy and take home. That's great too.

The point in all this is to improve your thinking and find new truth that will help you as a leader. Use a notebook to jot down ideas that solve current leadership challenges or opportunities you are facing.

Leaders often find some of their most important and favorite books this way. As author Mary Ann Schaffer said, "I have gone to [a specific bookshop] for years, always finding the one book I wanted—and then three more I hadn't known I wanted." Top leaders also rule out a lot of books that they might have read but probably didn't need to.

Step 3: Take One (or More) Home

As you go through these books and make some new friends, pay attention to which ones really ought to be permanent companions and additions to your family library. Choose the ones you need to write in and use. Put those in your shopping cart and buy them! Take them home and apply all the other leadership reading skills in this book.

This is a great exercise because it puts you in contact with a lot of ideas in quick succession. You can't help but come away with all sorts of nuggets. And you usually come away with some important and fun new titles to improve your list.

PART III
Leaders Are Readers

A truly good book teaches me better than to read it. I must soon lay it down, and commence living on its hint. What I began by reading, I must finish by acting.
—Henry David Thoreau

16

LOVE LEARNING

I declare after all there is no enjoyment like reading!
How much sooner one tires of anything than of a book!—
When I have a house of my own, I shall be miserable
if I have not an excellent library.
—Jane Austen

As we suggested with the motivational factor of getting to know your book, top leaders understand the importance of putting yourself in a position where you're excited and likely to read. In order to fully accomplish this, leaders find a way to make themselves fall deeply in love with learning.[16]

> Leaders find a way to make themselves fall deeply in love with learning.

Developing this love and becoming a hungry lifetime reader will make a huge difference in your success as a leader and in every other aspect of your life. As Orrin Woodward said, "Champions do consistently what others do sporadically."

> "Champions do consistently what others do sporadically."
> —Orrin Woodward

He also explained that people either hate changing enough to fail or hate failing enough to change and that the real leaders are those who pick the second option. While all of this is true, it's not just reading this quotation that makes all the difference in a potential leader's life. This is the kind of thinking that leads to leadership, but if a person never gets beyond thinking to action and results, he or she will never be a top leader.

To move from point A to point B, leaders know that they have to leverage this powerful information and thinking in their lives in order to actually bring results. They also understand that it's nobody's job but their own to make sure they actually do what they say they want to, or in this case, read what they know they should.

There are many ways to do this, and it will vary based on the personality and temperament of the individual reader. Here are a few things you can do to help create an environment for yourself where you not only read frequently but also thoroughly enjoy it— because true enjoyment is one of the best motivators for any reader.

Read the Right Books

One leader shared her story of how she developed a love for learning and keeps herself "in the zone" as a voracious leadership reader:

The principle I had to start with is to read all the time. This sounds funny because it doesn't make sense that reading a lot would make you want to read even more. Anyway, I was at a time in my life when I had several hours a day I could

> "I developed a habit of 'read until you feel like reading,' and that really worked for me."

dedicate to reading, and I knew it would make a difference, so I set out to do it.

At first, it could be difficult because I wasn't always "in the mood," but I developed a habit of "read until you feel like reading," and that really worked for me.

I've always been a very self-motivated person, and I rarely do things just because others want me to, but once I had committed myself, I started to see a real difference in my life. The way I made this work was: I started with books that were naturally appealing to me.

Honestly, whatever you pick up in the library, if you actually read it, is almost always a good start. As long as it isn't a trashy romance novel, it will almost always lead you to better and better reading. So that's what I did. I picked out books I liked, and I read them all the time.

After that, I tried pushing myself to read things that were a little bit out of my comfort zone but that were recommended by mentors or friends. I even enjoyed the challenge! I tried books that were more complex and harder as I went along.

Since I started at my level (but with a little push to be even better), I was able to enjoy the growing process and keep it steadily growing.

I went with that policy for several months, and eventually, I got to a place where I really did like reading—a lot. It became a real hobby for me, and it is very helpful in my life and career.

Once I had developed good habits of reading, and got to a place where I could honestly say I loved it, I moved on from the "read until you feel like it" motto and found one that's even better for me:

If I don't feel like reading, it's because:

1. I'm not reading the right books. (I'm either not pushing myself hard enough, and my inner hero is rebelling against my mediocrity; I'm trying to move too fast, and I'm so far above my level that everything is going over my head instead of making me think; or there's another book that I really need to read right now.)

Or

2. I shouldn't be reading right now. (There is something
   else in my life that I need to focus on, and I need to
   shut my book and make it happen before I resume.)

It's important not to go too easy on yourself when you're
deciding this. Obviously, the point isn't to find a good cop-
out; we're trying to be leaders! But as long as you're really
honest with yourself and commit to following through on
whichever one is *truly* right, you can't go wrong! (And you
can always come back to your book later.)

Read Different Books Differently

Another leader, with a very different background and personality,
shared the following bits of wisdom:

Different books are different.
Bottom line.
Once you understand that, it's hard to fathom why people
always try to read them the
same. It's obviously nonsensical.
It reminds me of Einstein's
definition of insanity ("doing
the same thing over and over
again and expecting different
results") but backwards, or
something.

> "If I try to read almost anything in the *real* world the way I used to read textbooks in school, I won't like it very much. And even if I did, it probably wouldn't help me very much."

If I try to read *The Seven
Habits of Highly Effective People*
the same way I try to read Plutarch's *Lives*, of course I'll have
a bad experience. Also, if I try to read almost anything in the
real world the way I used to read textbooks in school, I won't

like it very much. And even if I did, it probably wouldn't help me very much.

That's why most people hate reading. They're used to reading boring things in boring ways, so no matter what book they're opening, they go about it with bad expectations, bad habits, and a bad attitude. Most people never read a book after college? No kidding!

The trick is to be open and excited about what you're about to read (don't assume it'll be terrible, or it will), and approach it differently, depending on what it is.

Maybe when you read fiction, you start on page one and read straight through in one sitting; maybe you do it out loud, discussing it with your kids as you go.

And then with a self-help book, you read a section a day or read the introduction and the conclusion before the meat of the book.

Whatever you do, remember that you don't have to be bored for it to work—in fact, it *won't* work if you are!

I Have to Tell You about This!

Another aspiring leader shared this story about how her mentor helped her improve her reading habits and develop a hunger for reading:

> I remember for a long time, I felt like my reading wasn't really meaningful. I felt like the kid in high school struggling with math who asks his mom, "How am I ever going to use this in real life?"
>
> Obviously, that was very discouraging. So I decided to be bold and actually ask the question.
>
> I marched right up to one of my mentors and demanded, "Why do I have to read? I don't think reading is really needed for my life purpose; I can achieve my dreams without it. I

know some people need to read, but it just has nothing to do with what I care about."

He wasn't too surprised, since he had seen me struggling for weeks.

He calmly waited until I was finished before he asked, "Who are you sharing your thoughts and lessons with after you read?"

"Thoughts and lessons?" I responded heatedly. "You're implying that I have any of those! I told you I'm not really getting anything from the stuff I read, and I'm ready to stop now, so I can fill my time with something good."

I admit I wasn't having one of my more respectful days, and I was super burned out from feeling like I had no results.

That's when he decided I'd had enough time feeling like the know-it-all in the room.

"Lacy," he said, "I've known you long enough to know that you're never 'not having thoughts.' The really shocking part is that you don't seem to want to share them with anyone." *(I guess he thinks I'm a bit opinionated!)*

Anyway, after he finally calmed me down, he was able to remind me that I learn best when I have an outlet. I'm not one of those people who can just read something and learn everything I need to from it. My husband is like that; he reads and learns and grows and never needs anybody else. But not me.

I always have to discuss what I'm reading in order for me to really pull the important answers from it. So my mentor and I set up a regular time to discuss the things we were reading. He had a few other protégés who could use the discussion, he said, and he invited them as well.

It is amazing how talking about what I read changed things for me! I wasn't only excited about reading; I was on fire! I couldn't get enough out of the books I had on my shelves, so I had to get additional recommendations from my mentor and fellow discussers. And aside from reading a ton, I was gaining so much from my reading.

My friends always tease me that I like the sound of my own voice too much, but that's just the way I learn best. When I want to really internalize an idea and make it part of me, I have to *externalize* it by teaching it to others.

I know not everybody needs to have an outlet like that, discussing with other people and having an opportunity to really *teach* the principles they're learning, but if you're someone who *does* need it, you really can't do without it.

When you consider what a difference it will make on your motivation and your results, it's totally worth it to create this environment where you can get regular discussion and learning. It makes all the difference!

John Berry said it beautifully: "If your library is not 'unsafe,' it probably isn't doing its job." If you're not in danger of getting caught in your library for hours by a good and exciting book, either you or your library needs some improvement. And at least some of the books you read should really challenge you and help you grow.

> "If your library is not 'unsafe,' it probably isn't doing its job."
> —John Berry

As you make a point of putting yourself in an environment to love reading, you will find that your reading benefits you more and that you also do it more.

"Hate" What You Read

*I really hate those books where the murderer turns
out to be somebody you never heard of
who pops up in the last chapter.*
—Jane Haddam

One of the most off-the-wall principles of leadership reading is that it's not only acceptable to hate a book; it's great! That is, it's great if you do the right things with it.

Just like any other negative in life, books that you hate are opportunities. They can be used to teach you important lessons that will lead to all sorts of future victories, or they can be allowed to keep you from growing if you get too obsessed with things that don't matter.

> The leadership path is to make low points into launching platforms.

The leadership path is to make low points into launching platforms, and the way to achieve that with books you can't stand is to think about them enough to actually articulate the reasons for your dislike.

If you don't do this, you can easily be thrown into a state of personal discontentment with reading. If hating a book makes you give up reading, you have two big problems. First off, you'll stay unhappy because you'll never rise above the negative energy caused by your anger toward the book, and second, you'll probably be a better failure than you are a leader. Neither of these results is very good, and the alternative is powerful and exciting,

> If hating a book makes you give up reading, you have two big problems.

so we recommend the leadership reading approach to "terrible" books.

If you take the time to think about the hated book, discuss it with others who've read it, and compare it to some of the books you love, you'll find yourself in a much better place than if you never read it.

You should get excited whenever you or someone you mentor or work with really hates a book. As long as someone hates it, there's room for learning and growth because there's no apathy involved. The person who hates it is engaged in the conversation and has points to discuss.

> You should get excited whenever you or someone you mentor or work with really hates a book.

The first question you have to ask yourself in these situations is *why* you or the other person has a problem with the book.

Why Do You Hate It?

Did the book attack or challenge your core beliefs?

If so, you need to really learn who is right. Sometimes we have incorrect beliefs, and the process of correcting them is always painful. But it *is* necessary for true success.

On the other hand, you might be correct, and the author is wrong or deceived. If so, use it as an important educational debate where you learn the enemy's side, strengthen your own side, and ultimately discover how to defeat the enemy's wrong ideas. Better with a book than waiting for it to come up in real life.

An excellent example of this is Emma Cox's experience with Ayn Rand's *The Virtue of Selfishness*:

> When I was reading *The Virtue of Selfishness*, I didn't half know what to do with myself! I think she's brilliant in the way she sees human nature, and her logical progression is really excellent—until you get to the conclusion.
>
> It's strange to be reading something and agree with every point along the way but then find that the end result is totally skewed. It got really, really frustrating after a while! How can she think that A and B and C lead to . . . that?
>
> It's so annoying! You're reading along like, "Yes. Yes. Yes. Ye—what? How did that get in here? What on earth does this have to do with it?" I almost put it down because something was seriously wrong with it, but then my husband was like, "Why does she say that? If you agree with the basis of her argument but not her main point, there's probably a reason."
>
> Of course, I wasn't sure there was any reason in this; it seemed like ordered insanity but still totally mad. But then he asked me to prove that she was wrong. (Not that he agreed with her, but he knows when I'm intense about stuff I need to work through it, or I stay intense.)
>
> Anyway, I was about to start listing out why she was wrong, and I realized I wasn't sure. I knew that what I believed didn't match what she believed. But she had made a whole outline and series of essays on her point, and I didn't have a concise argument against her—it was mostly just emotional.
>
> So I set out to prove her wrong. I got to read a bunch of cool stuff by C. S. Lewis and Viktor Frankl, and both of those helped me understand my side of the debate.

But this whole thing taught me the power of reading what I used to call "crazy people's thoughts."

It was way better to learn this from a book and talking to my husband than in a debate with a real person in front of my children, or something. I wouldn't want them to think Rand's ideas are totally right just because I couldn't effectively say otherwise.

> It's one thing to learn from something that you agree with and to internalize it.…But sooner or later, you will meet with opposition—that's how leadership works—and practicing on books can get you in the best shape possible for a real fight.

It's one thing to learn from something that you agree with and to internalize it. That certainly makes you a stronger person and helps you achieve great things. But sooner or later, you will meet with opposition—that's how leadership works—and practicing on books can get you in the best shape possible for a real fight. This is extremely important and completely worth it.

Do you hate the book because it was stupid?

In that case, you should usually push yourself to dig deeper because there's frequently more there than you're seeing, and going through this process will be very good for your leadership abilities. When you think something is "stupid," the real problem is often that you are being lazy or closed-minded. Remember that in leadership reading, the important part is not just what the author wrote but what you think, learn, and discover. So when the book is "stupid," use your creativity, leadership, and problem-solving skills to make it better. "Stupid" shouldn't be a cop-out; it should be a challenge and an exciting project.

Is the book difficult to understand?

Sometimes we hate books because they're written in a way that doesn't make sense to us. Especially when we read older books and classics, we often find that many of the words are unfamiliar and the meaning of many sentences seems unclear.

People who try to dig into books like *The Federalist Papers*, for example, often dislike the experience because it's hard. This is a legitimate concern, and top leaders have to address it, or their leadership will suffer. It comes down to this: Top leaders have to do hard things. They have to face huge challenges and defeat big weaknesses, in themselves and

> It comes down to this: Top leaders have to do hard things. They have to face huge challenges and defeat big weaknesses, in themselves and others.

others. To be truly effective and excellent, they have to push through difficult books like *The Federalist Papers, Democracy in America, Pilgrim's Progress,* and others. In short, sometimes the answer is to suck it up—you'll be glad you did.

We do, however, have some words of encouragement for you. The books themselves may be difficult, but that doesn't mean your whole experience has to be frustrating. In fact, we believe in doing things the *best* way, not just the hardest.

So find a mentor! Get a group of friends together, and push through it together.

As mentioned in an earlier chapter, Chris Brady recommends making an outline of each chapter/section as you read along; basically synopsize the whole book as you go. This is a great way to make hard books easier, and it will also help you mentor others through it in the future.

You don't have to dislike or avoid things just because they're hard. You can be excited about all of the learning and growth that will come from really pushing yourself to accomplish important tasks.

When It's Worth It, It's Worth It

As you read these tough but truly fantastic books, remember that your hard work is not unnecessary, and it *is* worth it. Persevering will improve your leadership ability, and it will make reading the easier books that much better.

As you increase your own personal depth by reading truly deep works, you'll increase the depth of what you can get out of all the other books you read. This is incredibly helpful, as top leaders know.

> As you increase your own personal depth by reading truly deep works, you'll increase the depth of what you can get out of all the other books you read.

There are all sorts of other reasons why you might dislike what you're reading, but don't let them stop you from getting the most out of it. You've already spent the time on it, so that would just be a waste. When you don't like a book, get excited because you're about to learn a lot!

18

HEAL BROKEN STORIES

Reading without reflecting is like eating without digesting.
—Edmund Burke

Another reason that people sometimes dislike a book is that it left them feeling completely sad and depressed. We call this a "broken story."[17] In this case, there's another key to leadership reading that will help you get the most out of your reading experience: Figure out how to heal what's broken in the book. This is also a great way for leaders to practice and develop their problem-solving skills.

The title of this chapter might make it sound as if it only applies to fiction, but that isn't the case. Any book you read tells a story, even when it isn't obvious, and these stories aren't always whole or healthy. Often as you read, you'll find books that are missing huge chunks of knowledge or wisdom here or there, which makes them not only incomplete but incorrect. Others teach things that are downright wrong.

Take Control and Learn the Lessons

The lesson of leadership reading in these cases is to discuss, consider, deliberate, debate, and brainstorm—either by yourself or with a group of peers or associates—until you come up with a solution to the book's problem. In short, you discover what the book was missing and fix it.

By doing this, you learn to patiently and effectively recognize and solve important problems in a safe environment. You don't have to do this with every broken book, but when you do choose to do it, you're in for a powerful learning experience.

> You learn to patiently and effectively recognize and solve important problems in a safe environment.

This will improve your personal ability to self-correct. And it will also be helpful in your leadership because you'll be a well-trained problem-solver.

It will also help you with mentoring people because you'll have the necessary skills to improve your protégés' thinking and properly course-correct.

On top of these benefits, you'll be better able to approach others with a "complete, not compete" mentality, since you'll have more experience accepting things as they are, with weaknesses and flaws, and taking the steps necessary to improve, complete, and heal the situation.

You will encounter all sorts of broken stories in your life as well as in reading. By learning and practicing this skill, you are preparing yourself to appropriately and effectively face a number of relationships and challenges that will come to you as a leader.

19

LOOK FOR MENTORS IN BOOKS

Employ your time in improving yourself by other men's writings so that you shall come easily by what others have labored hard for.
—Socrates

Another great trait of top leaders is that they are constantly in search of qualified mentors to add to their list and help them on their path to success. Therefore, another important technique of leadership reading is looking for mentors in your readings.

When leaders look for mentors, they aren't just looking for the guy with the best credentials or the one with the biggest "Mentor" sticker on his forehead. Instead, they're looking for the person who has observable experience and tangible results—the person who can give them true mentoring.

Likewise, when you're looking for mentors in books, don't assume that it's always going to be the author who teaches you. Learn from the characters, from the heroes and the villains, the successes and the failures. In business books, for example, pay special attention to

> When you're looking for mentors in books, don't assume that it's always going to be the author who teaches you.

the stories. But make sure you don't discount the author as a potential mentor; judge on merit.

Emulate the strengths that brought success to characters like Jean Valjean[18] or Penelope,[19] real people like Gandhi and Margaret Thatcher, and authors such as Dale Carnegie or George S. Clason. Learn from a diverse list of people who have been successful in various aspects of life that you consider important.

Also, learn from the weaknesses and strengths of others, whether they are/were bad or good as individuals. Let the failures of people like Achilles,[20] St. Claire,[21] or Aaron Burr teach you what not to do. And learn from the strengths of leaders like Isaiah, Joan of Arc, Abraham Lincoln, Andrew Carnegie, Winston Churchill, and Martin Luther King Jr. By taking what you can from the life lessons of others, you are stocking up on valuable information that will help you get through yours with flying colors.

> By taking what you can from the life lessons of others, you are stocking up on valuable information that will help you get through yours with flying colors.

How Leaders Overcome the System

Bestselling author Paul Coelho claimed that "people never learn anything by being told; they have to find out for themselves," and in a way, he is right. However, reading the experiences of others who have found out for themselves, immersing yourself in their nuggets of truth and in their stories, is one way leaders have found to appropriately and effectively overcome the system. Because they're dedicated to learning the smart way (instead of always the hard way) and they know how to find mentors in books, leaders are frequently able to actually "find out for themselves" in the pages of a book.

As you learn from the examples of the people you read about, you will be better able to avoid painful failures and achieve meaningful successes.

By seeking out mentors from Scripture, history, literature, philosophy, and the powerful modern thinkers in self-help books and biographies, you will take advantage of the library of human experience and understanding, instead of fighting every battle on your own.

20

WORDS, WORDS!

*Words are, of course, the most powerful
drug used by mankind.*
—Rudyard Kipling

O ne technique of great leaders is to fall in love with words. That's right: words. Words are important. Words are central to greatness. And words are fun. They are incredibly powerful symbols. Great leaders understand how to use words effectively, and great mentors learn how to do this by first having fun with words.

> Words are central to greatness.

But how? Keep track of any new words that come along as you read. What we sometimes forget is that the author who wrote that huge, obscure, or new word in front of you didn't understand it either—until he did. The obviousness of this statement makes it seem ridiculous that we forget it, yet we do. Top leaders understand that before authors write the words in their books, at some point, they look them up in a dictionary or have them explained. Authors aren't born with an infinite understanding of the definition of every word ever. But they *do* fall in love with words and learn their meanings and nuances as they go along. At least, the most effective ones do this.

To apply this in your own reading, and stop forgetting the obvious, Chris Brady recommends a simple remedy: write new or interesting words you come across at the front of the book so you can look them up and become even more familiar with them later on.

When you're finished with the whole book, the following two-step exercise is a great way for you to gain further insight into each word:

1. Get an etymological dictionary, either in hard copy or online.

2. Select five words (from the list you made in the front of your book) and study their roots. Find something fun about each, and share it with somebody.

That's it. That's the whole project. After you've done this five times, you'll probably be hooked. Now just repeat the process whenever you want to know more about a word.

Writing this in the books you are reading is an excellent way to read like a top leader. Most people today tend to just skip past words they don't clearly understand, but not leaders. They stop and figure out what a word really means, including looking it up if needed.

> Stop and figure out what a word really means, including looking it up if needed.

And lots of leaders go the extra step and research the etymology of the word. Leaders know that words are vital to leadership, and they are excited about opportunities to increase their vocabularies, understanding, and wisdom.

Just Plain "Sincerely"

Some of the most valuable ideas about history come from letters of great people. In British history, letters are often closed with phrases such as the following: "I am, Sir, your most humble and obedient servant"; "I beg to remain, Sir, your most humble and obedient servant"; or "I remain, Sir, your faithful and obedient servant."

Many of the American founders followed this pattern. For example, George Washington frequently ended letters with "Your most obedient and most humble servant" and "Mrs. Washington joins me in compliments."

Over time, the most typical British responses became "Yours faithfully"; "Yours truly"; and "Yours sincerely." By contrast, in the United States the most popular endings are "Sincerely yours" and just plain "Sincerely."

This illustrates the way different people read. Students are often taught that there is a "right" way to write a letter and that the writer should put "Sincerely" at the end before his or her name.

Most readers simply skim past the "Sincerely" without even noticing. Even advanced readers often read "Sincerely" or "Yours faithfully" and note that the first was most likely an American writer, while the second was probably British. One online thread asked, "What does the phrase 'Sincerely yours' at the end of letters really mean?"

> "What does the phrase 'Sincerely yours' at the end of letters really mean?"

Answers from different people included the following:

> "It stands for that you are confident and thankful for the time and effort it takes for the person to respond to it, and that you are true in what you enclose in the letter."
>
> "Sincerely means genuinely."
>
> "It kind of means 'I like you like a friend' or something like that."

But top leaders read differently. For example, one successful business leader wanted to be sure he was using "Sincerely,"

"Sincerely yours," or the other options correctly in a letter that was important to him, so he didn't just skim it. He looked it up.

Roots Matter

He found that the root of the word *sincere* is important. In Latin, *sin* means without, and *cere* means wax. Roman sculptors would make stone sculptures and then try to sell them in the market. If the stone cracked, they would fill the cracks with wax and smooth it over to look good. Thus, a sculpture "without wax," or sincere, was one without deception—the real thing, with no wax covering hidden cracks.

That's a pretty good thing to put at the end of a letter: "No deception—the genuine article."

Top leaders understand words and meanings because they take the time to read works with words they don't know or clearly understand. In fact, many top leaders write down any new word they read or hear and make sure to look it up.

And, once you clearly understand the meaning, don't forget to write it in the margin next to the word.

21

Look for the Mystery

The possession of knowledge does not kill the sense of
wonder and mystery. There is always more mystery.
—Anais Nin

In his book *The Grace of Great Things*, Robert Grudin talks about three different kinds of learning, which he calls Task Learning, Problem Learning, and Mystery Learning.

Task learning is accomplished by doing assignments or by looking for specific "right" answers while reading. Problem learning occurs when a person is given a problem to solve or told to figure out the answer to something by reading a chapter, article, or book. In contrast, mystery learning takes you to an even deeper level because there's nobody there to tell you what you're looking for or whether you're even looking at all.

Aim High

The highest level of learning, and a vitally important aspect of leadership and leadership reading, is mystery learning. This means readers have to find a problem or task on their own before they can set themselves to solving or accomplishing it. In reading, *mystery* means that the reader has to figure

> The highest level of learning, and a vitally important aspect of leadership and leadership reading, is mystery learning.

out the hidden lessons in the course of reading. In fact, the author may not even have known that the lessons were there—but the reader must find them anyway.

As top leaders read, they are *looking* for a mystery, which is any idea that comes to them that helps them in their life. To do this, they must challenge assumptions, ask important questions, and grapple for difficult and uncharted answers while they read. By looking for mysteries, top leaders are able to argue with the author and themselves on deeper levels. They are thinking in powerful ways, and they are recognizing and overcoming challenges and problems they hadn't realized existed before they picked up the book.

English novelist Mark Haddon said, "Lots of things are mysteries. But that doesn't mean there isn't an answer to them." One of the goals of leadership readers should be to find the mysteries in each book, even the ones that don't seem to have any, and unlock the answers.

Keep an Eye Out

The way to accomplish this is to fully apply the other steps of leadership reading while also paying special attention to potential mysteries. Look for little discrepancies or subtle magnificence.

In short, we can find amazing answers to our questions in books if we'll openly seek hidden gems of knowledge and wisdom. This requires us to think, ponder, and deeply consider as we read. This is how top leaders read.

Oliver DeMille suggests that readers make sure to notice when there are deeper, underlying meanings or questions in the text. Watch for tasks, lessons, great quotations, and things you want to remember and teach to others; mysteries are often found in these places.

Sometimes the mysteries in a book are big problems that the reader has to solve, but not always. Sometimes the mystery in a book is a hidden treasure, an important question, a great footnote that recommends a new book, and so on.[22] Whatever it is, leadership readers can utilize the mystery to make themselves better, more effective leaders.

It's amazing how much you'll get by simply looking for deeper meaning. Sometimes you'll uncover mysteries the author intended to be found by more astute readers, and sometimes the mysteries will be inspired by your own thoughts and feelings.

Searching for the mystery within a book will bring your leadership reading to a higher level of success, which will mean your leadership abilities will be continually growing and improving.

22

READ ALOUD

Children are made readers on the laps of their parents.
—Emilie Buchwald

Reading aloud can be done in a variety of ways, and it is beneficial for a number of reasons. One of the most obvious reasons is simply to boost your own level of comprehension, depth, and connection with whatever you're reading. Often, when you read out loud, you catch things you wouldn't have otherwise and understand things in different, more powerful ways.

The auditory aspect of reading aloud—the fact that you're *hearing* the words as you read—can help you better connect, which will add depth and power to your experience, just like smelling the book before you read. The idea behind both is to get your whole brain involved in the process of reading.

For this reason, listening to the audio version of a book you've already read is a great way to reinforce it and add a level of depth to your understanding. The author (or reader) often puts emphasis on certain words or ideas in a way that makes the book come alive at a whole new level.

> When you read out loud, you have to add a new level of interpretation as you choose your tone, inflection, and emphasis.

On top of that, reading aloud will help you achieve a more active sort of reading because you're not just seeing and hearing the words as someone else wrote or spoke them; you're speaking them yourself.

When you read out loud, you have to add a new level of interpretation as you choose your tone, inflection, and emphasis.

The difference between active reading and passive reading is obvious, and one is clearly superior to the other in leadership reading.

The bottom line is this: Top leaders want to connect with their books on deep levels, having as much of their brain awake and involved in the process as possible. And they also want to be very active in their pursuit of greater knowledge and personal growth.

> Almost all top leaders got to where they are by taking responsibility for their own excellence and then playing an active role in making it happen.

Almost all top leaders got to where they are by taking responsibility for their own excellence and then playing an active role in making it happen. Reading aloud is one way to apply this principle to your reading.

Pass It On

There is another key aspect of reading aloud that top leaders understand and leverage. Top leaders know the importance of passing the habits of great leadership on to their children and grandchildren. You can be a great leader and mentor in the world, in your community, or in business, but you are less effective—and likely short-sighted—if you don't make a point of teaching your own children the important principles and techniques of real leadership.

That said, another way leaders use reading aloud to increase their leadership is by reading to their children to pass on great information and good habits.

Reading to your children helps them in a number of ways. For one, you're building and strengthening valuable relationships with your kids while everyone involved is simultaneously learning new and valuable life lessons from the book itself and the discussions that follow reading time.

Also, by setting the example, you're making reading an activity that's fun and cool in your family culture, which will make your children more likely to want to read on their own time as they grow older.

Aside from that, numerous studies have found that reading to children from a young age also increases their vocabulary and ability to think creatively, which are both really helpful for effective leadership.

And to add one more point (though, of course, there are countless other benefits), when you read to your children, you often allow them to learn and experience things that are still beyond their own reading level but not beyond their comprehension level.

One father shared a story about his nine-year-old daughter who was still reading at a nine-year-old level but was hungry for more than that. By investing in audiobooks and family reading time, he was able to help her study the subjects she was interested in and found that, within a few short months, he could quiz her on almost any person or event from history, and she had at least some factual knowledge and a personal opinion about the person or event in question.

This is an excellent illustration of why reading aloud or listening to audiobooks can make a significant difference in the lives and education of your children. You can give a girl with a nine-year-old vocabulary and reading level a vast knowledge base that would otherwise be beyond her reach. And all the while, you're building stronger relationships and creating a family culture that is in itself a legacy of leadership and excellence. This is one of the most important things a leader can do to influence future leadership and freedom.

Top leaders understand that part of their role is to mentor other upcoming leaders. Often, this includes protégés and mentees who come up in their business or leadership roles, and that's great. But one big way for current leaders to seriously hurt future leadership is for them to ignore the responsibility they have to mentor the coming generation that lives in their own homes.

> Top leaders understand that part of their role is to mentor other upcoming leaders.

Reading and Relationships

Leaders should take seriously the relationships they have with their own children. Reading aloud to your children today can considerably improve your own leadership influence and effectiveness while also safeguarding the future.

Not only is this a vital leadership trait; it's something you owe to your children and grandchildren—and also to your parents and grandparents. Leaders can honor the sacrifice and excellence of past generations by truly embracing their own responsibility to raise and cultivate future generations. Thinking generationally in this way will help you accomplish great things, including your own important life purpose.

Reading aloud, either to yourself or your children, is one of the best ways to make your reading have an impact *right now*, today, as well as in the future.

READ AND REREAD

If one cannot enjoy reading a book over and over again,
there is no use in reading it at all.
—Oscar Wilde

Rereading books is a controversial topic in many circles. Some people think it's a waste of time. For them, the goal is all about reading as *many* books as possible. Others think it's the best thing possible—why waste your time on untried books? Overall, it's something about which everyone (at least among those who read at all) seems to have an opinion, and there's little agreement on what's right or best.

Interestingly, this disagreement is significantly smaller in leadership reading. Why? Because almost all top leaders agree that there's a very important place for rereading the best books. Obviously, they prefer not to waste their time rereading books that weren't worth their time in the first place. And some books might be good once, but once is enough. But in either case, they can agree that there are other books they would read again and again.

There are many reasons for rereading books, but before we get into that, let's get really clear on exactly *which* books you should actually be rereading.

What to Reread

The easy thing about deciding which books to reread is that you've already read them all. You know which ones were good and which ones really weren't. The hard part is being really honest with yourself and being certain to reread the ones you should reread instead of giving in to the temptation to only read the easy or fun ones.

> The easy thing about deciding which books to reread is that you've already read them all. You know which ones were good and which ones really weren't.

Not that you shouldn't have fun rereading—you definitely should, whenever possible—but this shouldn't be your only priority. As you're looking at your bookshelves trying to select a good reread, ask yourself the following questions:

1. Was it a good book?

2. Did it change me?

3. Did it inspire powerful action in me?

4. Am I better for having read it?

5. Can I learn anything more from it?

6. Are there certain parts I need to read again? (Remember, since this is about impact, you don't have to read the book linearly—especially on a reread. Just read the parts that matter to you right now.)

7. Which parts of the book should I reread, and in what order?

8. What other books should I read at the same time to maximize my experience? (This question assumes you will

be rereading, but it can make a difference in your decision-making process.)

9. Will my time be best spent rereading this book or something else? If something else, what? (Be sure to find a specific replacement. It's usually better to be reading something than not to read because you're waiting for the right book to come along. The "right" book usually comes when you're reading something that's just "good.")

10. Am I the same person I was when I last read this book, or am I different? (If you've changed at all, there's a good chance you could get more out of the book than you did before.)

Answering these questions will usually help you decide which books should be reread. And understanding the following reasons for rereading will help you with the tougher decisions.

Tried-and-True

Italo Calvino said, "A classic is a book that has never finished saying what it has to say." By that definition, classics should certainly be reread because one reading can never give you everything, and as long as you're getting more from the book, it's worth reading. In fact, if you have a book you've read before and you know you have more to learn from it, reading it is often better than trusting luck and hoping to find another book of equal value. Since a previously read book will have your old notes—and possibly other people's—it's almost impossible for you to find one that will teach you quite as much.

> "A classic is a book that has never finished saying what it has to say."
> —Italo Calvino

Extra Depth

Often as you reread something, you'll actually notice different things in the text than you did before. Sometimes you'll find that your eyes skipped over things or that you misunderstood them the first time through, but on rereading them, you understand them differently.

Also, the fact that you know where the book is headed often allows you to notice things you didn't previously realize were significant. It's like when you watch a movie for a second time and you notice all those little foreshadowing events that first-time viewers don't even see.

In this way, rereading will help you achieve greater depth in your reading and better understanding of the valuable nuggets of truth that are sometimes hidden in the pages.

A New and Better You

Clifton Fadiman said, "When you reread a classic, you do not see more in the book than you did before; you see more in you than was there before." As we just discussed, you often *do* see more in the book with each new read, but this comment adds an interesting point to the conversation.

> You'd be a pretty strange person if you could manage to read a book over, even if you started the day after you finished, without having changed personally between reads.

One of the most important aspects in impactful rereading is your own personal growth *between* readings. You'd be a pretty strange person if you could manage to read a book over, even if you started the day after you finished, without having changed personally between reads. At the very least, you'll have different questions, concerns, goals, and intentions, and you probably will have read several books, overcome various challenges, achieved some victories, and faced a few defeats since the last time you read the book.

And because you're different, you can't help but have a new experience. Adding the thoughts and impressions that come with the "new you" to the words of the old you(s) and the author will make the book that much better! And you'll learn more.

24

STICKY NOTES AND DOG-EARS

No matter how little money and how few possessions
you own, having a dog makes you rich.
—Louis Sabin

One of the main reasons writing in your books is so valuable is that doing so makes it much easier to find important thoughts and concepts when you come back to a book years after you first read it. Since leaders often use books they read to help them prepare and support speeches they give or pieces they write, being able to find key passages and quotations is essential. That said, one way you can increase your ability to do this is to mark the most important pages with sticky notes or Post-it Flags or by folding down the corners. This allows you to really own your book and your learning process.

The Right Balance

Leaders who attempt to memorize every good word they ever read will find their opportunity for extensive reading severely weakened. When will they find the time to read if they spend their lives memorizing? On the other hand, if you don't retain anything from a book and can't find the information you need to remember later on, you'll end up wasting time on unnecessary rereading. In short, you have to find the right balance between memorizing every word and *losing* every word the moment you put the book down. As is often the case, top leaders accomplish this balance by leveraging a tried-and-true system: marking their books in such a way that they'll know how to find what they need.

It's the simplest thing in the world to turn down the corners of key pages as you read along, and it saves you the trouble of having to search through the entire book to find one important sentence. Or, if you are concerned about potentially damaging the pages and prefer to put in a sticky note, that works well too. We like a combination of both.

Systems Save Time

Whatever you decide, create a system that works for you, and use it in everything you read. It can be as complex as a color-coordinated sticky-note plan where you know what type of quotation or passage each color is marking or as simple as making a dog-ear on a page you think might be useful in the future.

> It can be as complex as a color-coordinated sticky-note plan where you know what type of quotation or passage each color is marking or as simple as making a dog-ear on a page you think might be useful in the future.

Either way, you're significantly reducing the number of pages you have to check for the quotation or concept you want. This allows you to spend your time on more valuable tasks and also to easily find what you need in your books.

Chris Brady recommends turning up the page from the bottom for really important pages. This puts a whole new emphasis on these things.

Marking pages will make you a much more effective reader because—like writing in your books—it allows you to learn and benefit from a book again, and again in the long term, instead of just while you're reading it.

25

BUNDLING

A single twig breaks, but a bundle of twigs is strong.
—Tecumseh

Sometimes as you finish a book, you'll be left with the feeling that you need more. Whatever plan or booklist you have set up for your next readings, you should really pay attention to these impressions. If you finish a book and it doesn't seem to be finished with you, stop and consider how to work with it.

> Bundling your books can be a great way to answer important questions and solve big problems in your life.

Interestingly, bundling is something that most of us know about but generally forget to do. Well, here's your reminder. Bundling your books can be a great way to answer important questions and solve big problems in your life. Although reading several books on various topics all at once can be an extremely valuable method of leadership reading, sometimes it's good to spend time studying deeply into a single topic or idea.

Three Types of Bundling

There are three main ways you can bundle your readings. The first (also the most commonly known and the easiest) is to bundle by *author*. Specifically, when you finish a book and want more like it, it's easy to jump on your favorite online bookstore, such as amazon.com or life-leadership-home.com, and type in the author's name. If he or she has written other titles, this should bring up a list of them. All you have to do is pick the one that sounds best and get to work! When you've finished the next book on the author's list, you can decide whether you want to go deeper or if it's time to move on.

The second type of bundling is by *topic*. This is a little more difficult, but it certainly isn't hard. And it can bring great results to your learning and reading. An easy way to do this is to go to amazon.com and search for the book you just finished. Amazon has a cool feature that provides a selection of the other books past buyers bundled with that one. Look for the section with the heading "Customers Who Bought This Item Also Bought." Peruse through these titles and take note of anything that catches your eye.

And finally, the third type of bundling is by *title*. This one takes the most creativity on your part but often brings the best results. To bundle by title, go to your favorite online bookseller, or even go in person to a brick-and-mortar bookstore, and just play around searching for variations on the title of the book you just finished.

For example, one reader finished *The ONE Thing* by Gary Keller and Jay Papasan and wanted to find out what others had to say about the same ideas, so he pulled out his laptop and went online. He started by typing in the title itself and scrolling through the search results. This all by itself brought up several good options for bundling, including:

1. *The One Thing You Need to Know: . . . About Great Managing, Great Leading, and Sustained Individual Success* by Marcus Buckingham

2. *One Big Thing: Discovering What You Were Born to Do* by Phil Cooke

3. *Decide One Thing: The One Thing EVERY Executive Team Must Decide* by Dave Ramos

And the list goes on.

After the reader picked the ones he wanted, he started to search different things that had to do with the original title.

Have Fun!

When he searched the word *one*, he added a few more to his list, and typing just the numeral *1*, he found *1: How Many People Does It Take to Make a Difference?* by Dan Zadra and Kobi Yamada, as well as *The 10x Rule* by Grant Cardone. And finally, he found Stephen Covey's *First Things First* by searching the word *first*.

So just have fun with it! Look at your title and make stuff up! You'll find lots of interesting books this way. Remember, you don't know what you don't know, and many of these books will be ones you've never heard of and never would have thought to look for.

> Just have fun with it! Look at your title and make stuff up! You'll find lots of interesting books this way.

Bundling is powerful! It not only gives you needed depth on important topics and ideas, but it also helps you find books that will increase your leadership effectiveness—books that wouldn't have come up if you hadn't gone looking.

26

Go Great or Go Home

*It is what you read when you don't have to that determines
what you will be when you can't help it.*
—Oscar Wilde

Orrin Woodward and Oliver DeMille wrote in their book
LeaderShift:

When most business leaders think of literature, they
think of Jane Austen, *Jane Eyre,* and all that. But what do
you think literature actually is? It's the history of how to
effectively spin things. It teaches how the greatest storytellers
of history got the masses to agree with them.

For example, Jane Austen convinced the masses that
they were just as important as the aristocrats, and that wit,
character, and doing the right thing even in hard situations
is what makes people great—not birth, social class, money,
or education. She was one of the original proponents of
performance over bureaucracy, credentialism, and elitism.
Literature is powerful, and it is the language of the masses.

Of course, the mass language of Jane Austen's day isn't the
mass language of the masses today. But popular authors in
each time period are popular precisely because they catch the
imagination of the people. It's helpful for thinking leaders to
look at popular literature as an important and effective way
of understanding the greater populace.

In our specialized modern world, most leaders aren't trained to think of it this way, but it's an interesting way to look at things. Steve Jobs was reported in the *New York Times* as being a lifetime student of the writings of William Blake, and Visa founder Dee Hock put writers like John Steinbeck and Wallace Stegner to similar use. Eventually, Hock came to consider Omar Khayyám's *Rubáiyát* the most helpful work of literature.

> "Popular authors in each time period are popular precisely because they catch the imagination of the people."
> —Orrin Woodward and Oliver DeMille

Nike founder Phil Knight also built a large personal library of literature and poetry. In his book *First Things First,* Stephen Covey called this consistent approach of learning leadership from the great books by its own title: wisdom literature.

Effective leadership readers—and, indeed, effective leaders—should utilize the wisdom literature of history to make themselves more influential and impactful in everything they do as well as better prepared for the tasks they will be required to do.

A Foundation for Leadership

Naturally, there are many great books for leaders to read, including ones that haven't been written yet. As you read great books using the techniques and tools of effective leadership reading, you'll be laying the foundation for excellent problem solving, communication, and leadership.

One way to help yourself consistently read great books is to join a monthly book club or monthly book subscription. Great reading never ends, and consistency in reading is one of the most important habits of top leaders.

To become a top leader, or to remain one, make reading a part of your daily life. By using the leadership reading techniques in this book, you can make reading more fun and effective and a powerful tool for achieving your potential and your most important goals.

27

BUILDING A PERSONAL LIBRARY

The very existence of libraries affords the best evidence
that we may yet have hope for the future of man.
—T. S. Eliot

Another important thing leaders can do throughout their lives to increase their leadership ability and influence and leave a powerful legacy for future leaders is to build a personal library. This means making a point of purchasing books you intend to read whenever possible. It also means reading and writing in them repeatedly and holding on to them, especially those that have had the biggest impact on your life.

Obviously, you won't be building anything if you spend a bunch of money on books that you proceed to throw away or send to the thrift store. You actually have to create a collection of books that you are constantly adding to in both numbers and value (by purchasing more and also rereading and writing in the ones you have).

There are three main reasons why you should be building your own library, rather than relying on a neighbor's collection or your local public library.

Access

The first is *accessibility*. If you have the books sitting in a room, just waiting for you to come pick them up when you need them, your experience will be much more efficient and effective than if you have to track them down each time you want something from them. You'll do a lot more marking and rereading.

In fact, if you did have to go out of your way each time, you might repeatedly sacrifice your important question or impression rather than find the book that holds your answer. And the bottom line is that this is a wholly unnecessary sacrifice, and it will hurt your growth and leadership in the long run.

By having the books you've read or should be reading accessible and ready for you whenever you need them, you'll be a lot more likely to use them when the need seems relatively small. After all, those relatively small needs are often the ones that lead to profound insight or pivotal understanding and improvement.

For example, Orrin Woodward discovered how much he relied on having his books close when he began living in two homes, spending summers in Michigan and winters in Florida. Eventually, he realized that he needed to put off some projects until summer (because his Michigan library had the books he needed for them) and others until winter (because the books he needed for those were in his Florida library). Having their books close is important to top leaders.

It's okay if this library includes some electronic and audiobooks too, but it should certainly have printed ones as well, since they're often more permanent and frequently more beneficial.

Availability

Along with all of this, according to Chris Brady, you should dedicate a small portion of your library and library fund to having a stock of books to give to people to assist them with their problems, challenges, or concerns. Leaders often help people address their issues by giving them books. So you should maintain a supply of the ones you most often need for this purpose. This is your "handout stockpile."

As you read, pay attention to which books you need to get duplicate copies of for your handout stockpile, and keep those books ready for people who come to you with questions. You'll probably be continuously adding to this stash (both in new titles and in replacements for those you give away) as well as depleting it by passing books to those who really need them. That's great! That is exactly why you have it, so don't be afraid to keep it in constant and fluid motion.

This is part of what Brady and Woodward call Level 5 Leadership: developing leaders who are continually developing other leaders.

Legacy

As we touched on earlier, a personal library is one of the best and most valuable legacies a leader can leave to his or her children, protégés, and future leaders. By creating a library with all sorts of extra notes and thoughts included in it, you are leaving future readers with an improved ability to learn the important principles and lessons of leadership and life, which will in turn help them to more effectively face their own challenges and difficulties and turn them into leadership opportunities.

A personal library that's actually been read and used by one or many readers is virtually irreplaceable. There's simply no way to go out and buy its equal at your local bookstore. In a way, used and marked-up libraries capture numerous mentors and volumes of mentoring advice that will help readers understand things on a level that someone reading the same books from a public library simply won't ever experience.

The people you help with your handout stockpile and the future readers who benefit from your notes and books will be a legacy of leadership and excellence that is truly priceless.

In short, creating a library is like encapsulating all your hard work and effort as a leadership reader and allowing future readers to start where you left off, instead of starting back at the beginning. As they try to reach the stars, they will be, as Newton suggested, standing on the shoulders of giants.

END WITH A BETTER PLAN

We have too many high sounding words and too few actions that correspond with them.
—Abigail Adams

Possibly the number-one skill of top leaders is that they take the important information, principles, and concepts they learn from their studies and their experiences and apply them to future action. As Orrin Woodward says, they "don't mistake thinking for action." Obviously, you can be the smartest guy on the planet and know everything there is to know, but if you never do anything with your knowledge, it won't do you or anyone else any good. Top leaders understand that when they learn new principles or techniques, they have to act on those new ideas in order for them to be worth anything.

In addition, they have to watch their actions to be sure those actions are bringing the right kind of results. This is absolutely crucial to effective leadership reading. If you aren't acting on the things you read in this book when you read other books, you probably won't see many of the

> Top leaders understand that when they learn new principles or techniques, they have to act on those new ideas in order for them to be worth anything.

valuable benefits of reading like a top leader. For that matter, if you don't take the knowledge and insights you gain from other books and let them change you in meaningful ways, you're missing many opportunities to significantly improve your leadership and life.

To be an effective leadership reader and a top leader, you have to take right thinking and turn it into right action, which will bring you the right results. Carl Jung said, "You are what you do, not what you say you'll do." To be a top leader, you have to understand that while these principles, ideas, and techniques can help you in your journey, you will ultimately have to do the work that will get you there.

> "You are what you do, not what you say you'll do."
> —Carl Jung

Finding mentors and books that will help you avoid unnecessary difficulties is just plain smart, but don't let that fool you into thinking that reading this or any other book is enough all on its own. Use books and mentors to help you define what you want to achieve and learn the best ways to go about doing it. But ultimately, *you* have to go out and *do*. This is another quality that separates top leaders from merely educated individuals. Top leaders leverage the information they get and use it to accomplish great things. They seek wisdom, they find it, and then they take action.

Preparation versus Perfectionism

As you do this, be sure to recognize the difference between needed preparation and perfectionist excuses. Leaders know that proper preparation makes action more impactful and more likely to achieve desired results. However, if they had waited to act whenever they thought they could be missing any piece of the puzzle, they wouldn't be top leaders today.

Don't wait till you're "ready" to take action. Start reading now and improve as you go. In reality, you will never be ready for what's ahead of you as a top leader unless you take the leap. There are some things that simply can't be taught, except through experience.

You will learn as you go. To paraphrase top leadership speaker Laurie Woodward, if the first thing you ever do as a leader goes perfectly, you waited way too long to do something.[23] Leaders understand this concept, and they act on it—which is precisely the point. As a leader, when you understand something, you act on it. Period. That's what leadership reading is all about.

In fact, this is so powerful that throughout history, whenever a dictator or tyrant has taken over a nation, one of the new ruler's first actions has typically been to burn the great books and imprison or kill the top leaders. Dictators know the profound influence of top leaders who read the way we have outlined in this book. This kind of reading, called *sensus plenior* or leadership reading, makes regular people into leaders—and leaders are dangerous to those who want to control everything.

> As a leader, when you understand something, you act on it. Period.

Most people don't understand how powerful this kind of reading really is, but history makes it clear that political and business leaders do know how significant leadership reading can be. Interestingly, this power comes merely from doing the simple techniques we've discussed here. Leadership reading is incredibly potent.

So, at the end of this book and every book you read, spend some valuable time debriefing the book by creating a new and improved plan. You began the book with a plan, which we hope helped you learn the right things from your reading. But by ending with an upgraded plan, you will be able to do even more of the right things with your reading.

In short, when you finish a book, pick up your list of questions and your beginning plan and add the principles you need to pull out of the book and how you intend to apply them. Put this in writing. Make an outline. Plan it all out. And then act on it.

Once your new plan is in motion, relax, grab another good book, and keep reading! You're on the path of leadership.

There are worse crimes than burning books.
One of them is not reading them.
—Ray Bradbury

NOTES

[1] William Shakespeare, *Hamlet*.

[2] Ibid.

[3] Jane Austen, *Northanger Abbey*.

[4] Grant Cardone, *The 10X Rule*.

[5] Gary Chapman, *The 5 Love Languages*.

[6] Arbinger Institute, *Anatomy of Peace*.

[7] Oliver DeMille, *A Thomas Jefferson Education*.

[8] Lewis Carroll, *Alice's Adventures in Wonderland*.

[9] Laurence J. Peter, *Peter's Quotations: Ideas for Our Time*.

[10] LIFE Leadership Essentials Series, *Financial Fitness*.

[11] Allan Bloom, *The Closing of the American Mind*.

[12] Claude Hamilton, *Toughen Up!*

[13] 1995 six-hour BBC production of Jane Austen's *Pride and Prejudice*.

[14] Cardone.

[15] Chris Brady, "The Beginning Vital Behaviors."

[16] DeMille.

[17] See *The Healing Power of Stories* by Daniel Taylor.

[18] Victor Hugo, *Les Misérables*.

[19] Homer, *The Odyssey*.

[20] Ibid.

[21] Harriet Beecher Stowe, *Uncle Tom's Cabin*.

[22] Oliver DeMille, *19 Apps*.

[23] Orrin and Laurie Woodward, "Building Teams and Understanding Leaders."

Other Books in the
LIFE Leadership Essentials Series

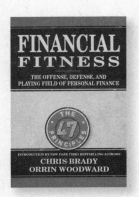

***Financial Fitness: The Offense, Defense, and Playing Field of Personal Finance* – $21.95**

If you ever feel that you're too far behind and can't envision a better financial picture, you are so WRONG! You need this book! The *Financial Fitness* book is for everyone at any level of wealth. Just like becoming physically or mentally fit, becoming financially fit requires two things: knowing what to do and taking the necessary action to do it. Learn how to prosper, conserve, and become fiscally fantastic. It's a money thing, and the power to prosper is all yours!

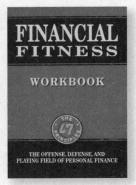

***Financial Fitness Workbook* – $7.95**

Economic affairs don't have to be boring or stressful. Make managing money fun in a few simple steps. Use this workbook to get off to a great start and then continue down the right path to becoming fiscally fabulous! Discover exactly where all of your money actually goes as you make note of all your expenditures. Every page will put you one step closer to financial freedom, so purchase the *Financial Fitness Workbook* today and get budgeting!

***Mentoring Matters: Targets, Techniques, and Tools for Becoming a Great Mentor* with Foreword by Orrin Woodward – $19.95**

Get your sticky notes ready for all the info you're about to take in from this book. Do you know what it means to be a *great* mentor? It's a key part of successful leadership, but for most people, the necessary skills and techniques don't come naturally. Educate yourself on all of the key targets, techniques, and tools for becoming a magnificent mentor with this easy-to-apply manual. Your leadership success will be forever increased!